DISCOVER THE POWER OF YOUR IPAD

ANOTHER COMPREHENSIVE GUIDE IN THE SERIES: FOR USERS OF ALL LEVELS—SIMPLIFYING TECHNOLOGY FOR A BETTER EXPERIENCE WITH LARGE PRINT AND ILLUSTRATIONS

RON BEHRMAN

TABLE OF CONTENTS

INTRODUCTION

You may not be aware of the vast possibilities that your iPad offers. Have you ever thought about how much more you can accomplish with your device? It's time to remove the restrictions and make your iPad fully functional. Welcome to your journey toward mastery. I'll be your guide and will go with you each step of the way.

Let's begin by talking about a shocking reality: Many iPad owners are still unaware of the myriad possibilities that exist within their gadgets. If you haven't been taking advantage of the amazing features and functionalities that can completely change your iPad experience, it's not your fault. In reality, research has revealed that a sizable portion of iPad owners only use a small portion of what their tablet is capable of, but that's different now.

I'm here to provoke thought in you by posing challenging questions. Are you aware that your iPad may serve as your go-to work tool, entertainment center, communication lifeline, study buddy, health tracker, and even travel assistant? It's time to discover the secrets and advance your iPad usage.

I am aware of the challenges and pain spots you may be experiencing with your iPad as we travel together. Because of this, I'm determined to face them head-on and make sure you acquire the information and abilities required to meet any obstacles. In fact, my commitment to meeting your specific needs as a user has led to the creation of this book.

You might be familiar with my earlier writing, which explored the complexities of Apple's environment in a book that was well-received by many readers. I'm here today with a new goal: a second book that is exclusively dedicated to the iPad, a gadget that demands all of our undivided attention. I want to empower you and give you the keys to unlocking this incredible device's hidden potential by focusing a whole book on it.

Let's now examine the advantages you might expect from these pages. This is more than just a book; it's a guide to the shortcuts, methods, and tactics that will revolutionize the way you use your iPad. The Life Mapping Method, a special framework I created to assist you in efficiently navigating the functions of your iPad, is at the heart of this manual.

Imagine increasing your productivity, managing your duties with ease, and applying effective apps to speed up your job. You'll learn how to incorporate your iPad into your everyday activities using the Life Mapping Method, making it a priceless tool in your pursuit of effectiveness and success.

The advantages don't stop there, either. We'll delve deeply into the entertainment category and examine innovations that will transform how you watch movies, listen to music, play games, and more on your iPad. We'll learn the connectivity and communication tricks that will keep you in touch with friends, family, and coworkers all over the world.

Another place where your iPad might excel is in education. Utilizing its features will give you access to a variety of information, instructional apps, and interactive tools that will improve your learning process. Your iPad can be used to broaden your horizons and develop new talents, from language study to online classes.

Your health is important as well. We'll look at how your iPad can aid in your quest for better health by monitoring your physical development, giving you access to wellness and meditation apps, and assisting you in forming positive lifestyle habits that will improve your general well-being.

Do you enjoy traveling frequently, or do you have any wanderlust? Your iPad can be the best travel companion possible, giving you access to navigational aids, language translators, and travel guides that will make your journey seamless and unforgettable.

Along with these important topics, we'll go into significant subjects like data privacy and safety to provide you with the knowledge you need to protect your information. We'll also look at senior-specific accessibility features that will make using your iPad accessible and convenient. Last but not least, we'll dig into the realm of iPad accessories and related Apple gear to help you optimize your tablet and utilize its features to the fullest.

As we travel together through this book, I want you to picture yourself living in a world where your iPad is a trusted companion who helps you achieve your objectives, discover your hobbies, and savor every moment. By the time you get to the last page, you'll have outperformed even the most seasoned iPad users, turning into a true expert on how to use its capabilities to improve your life.

It's important to trust someone with the experience and knowledge to lead the way when selecting a guide for this transformative journey. I've worked in IT for more than 50 years and have personally seen how technology has changed. My mission has always been to reduce the barrier between complicated technology and common consumers by offering user-friendly guidelines that enable people to get the most out of their mobile devices. You are in capable hands as we explore your iPad's full potential, so don't worry.

If you're a senior or a novice looking to learn how to use an iPad effectively and improve your experience, this book is for you. We will overcome obstacles, dismantle restrictions, and reveal the amazing opportunities that are waiting for you.

Are you, therefore, prepared to start on this ground-breaking journey? Prepare to unleash the hidden potential of your iPad, take command of your online existence, and embrace a life enhanced by technology.

1

THE IPAD—YOUR FIRST STEPS TOWARD A MODERN DIGITAL LIFESTYLE

Being connected and knowledgeable about technological changes is essential in today's digital society. The iPad has established itself as a flexible tablet, fusing the finest features of smartphones and PCs. The use, features, and numerous iPad models are all covered in detail in this chapter, along with other pertinent information. The necessity of embracing technology is highlighted by the rising demand for tablets. You can explore the digital environment and take advantage of its advantages by comprehending the iPad and its possibilities. This chapter gives you the information you need to make wise choices and make the most of the iPad's potential, whether you're a prospective purchaser or want to advance your knowledge. Let's start this adventure of exploration into the world of iPads.

A LOOK INTO THE ICONIC APPLE TABLET

What Is an iPad?

The iPad is a ground-breaking tablet computer created by Apple Inc. It provides a variety of features and functionalities that address different facets of our daily lives. The iPad has developed into a versatile companion that improves our experiences in a variety of life domains, from work and communication to education, entertainment, health, and travel:

Productivity: The iPad offers a variety of productivity tools and apps that help users manage chores, stay organized, and work more effectively. The iPad enables users to write and edit documents, spreadsheets, and presentations while on the go, thanks to its strong processing capabilities and user-friendly interface. It supports both well-known third-party programs like Microsoft Office and Google Suite as well as productivity programs from Apple like Pages, Numbers, and Keynote. The iPad offers a portable and feature-rich platform for work-related tasks, which can dramatically increase your productivity, whether you're a student, professional, or business owner.

Communication: The iPad allows for smooth communication thanks to its built-in camera and microphone. Through programs like FaceTime, Skype, and Zoom, users may keep in touch with friends and family, have video conversations, and take part in online meetings. The iPad also provides email clients, social media platforms, and messaging apps, allowing users to keep in touch and have meaningful interactions through a variety of channels.

Education: The iPad's dynamic and immersive learning environments have changed the educational landscape. For students of all ages, it provides a wide selection of instructional apps, ebooks, and digital content. Learning is made more interesting and accessible for students by the ease with which they may access textbooks, informational resources, and educational materials. Because of the flexibility of the iPad, teachers may design engaging classes, tests, and assessments that promote a more participatory and tailored learning environment.

Entertainment: The iPad has endless entertainment options available to it. With spectacular graphics and engrossing audio, customers may enjoy movies, TV shows, music, and games on this portable entertainment device. With Netflix, Apple Music, and Apple Arcade available as streaming services, the iPad opens up a world of limitless entertainment possibilities. In addition, those who enjoy digital art, photography, and graphic design will find the iPad to be the perfect platform because of its expansive, high-resolution display.

Health: The iPad is becoming a more useful tool in the healthcare industry. Users can track their physical activity, keep track of their sleep habits, manage their nutrition, and even interact with medical specialists through telehealth services with the aid of specialized health and fitness applications. The accessibility characteristics of the iPad also make it a useful tool for people with special needs, supporting rehabilitation, cognitive growth, and communication.

Travel: With features that make traveling easier, the iPad makes a practical travel companion. It makes it simpler to explore new places by providing access to navigational tools, language translation apps, and travel planning apps. Long flights or long commutes can be made more bearable for customers thanks to the iPad's extended battery life and portable design. The iPad's camera also makes it possible for users to record and share their travel memories in high-quality images and movies.

Who Is the iPad for?

The iPad is a flexible gadget that may be used by a variety of people, each with different requirements and preferences. Let's examine the various user types most likely to buy an iPad and the ways in which this amazing technology improves their lives:

- **Students**: Students of all ages can greatly benefit from the iPad. It is the perfect companion for taking notes, conducting research, studying, and even using digital textbooks because of its portability, interactive features, and accessibility to educational apps. Students can unleash their creativity and maintain organization throughout their academic careers with features like Apple Pencil compatibility and potent productivity tools.
- **Personal or Casual Use**: Many people use the iPad for daily activities and personal leisure. The iPad has a simple interface and a variety of entertainment alternatives, whether you're browsing the internet, streaming films, reading ebooks, or playing games.
- **Professionals**: The iPad, which provides efficiency and ease, has found a niche in a

number of professions. The iPad helps professionals like corporate executives, consultants, and entrepreneurs be more productive while on the go. It makes it possible for professionals to stay connected and productive no matter where they are with apps for email, document editing, project management, and video conferencing.

- **Designers and artists**: The iPad and Apple Pencil have completely changed the way that people create. Powerful drawing and design tools may help artists and designers sketch, paint, and produce digital artwork with accuracy and flow. They can easily work on the go or in a variety of creative settings thanks to the iPad's portability.
- **Gamers**: The iPad offers an intense gaming experience that appeals to gamers. The device offers console-like graphics and gameplay because of its powerful chipset and large game library. The iPad offers a fun gaming experience, whether it's simple puzzle games or titles with lots of graphics.
- **Musicians**: The iPad is a useful tool for musicians thanks to its extensive selection of music-making apps and virtual instruments.

The iPad gives artists the freedom to express their ideas and perform their music anywhere, from writing and recording music to practicing and giving performances.

- **Medical Professionals**: The iPad has made its way into the medical industry, giving doctors, nurses, and other healthcare workers crucial tools. It functions as a portable resource for medical literature, medical record-keeping, communication, and, in some circumstances, even as a diagnostic tool.

- **Travelers**: The iPad makes a great traveling companion. It is a practical travel companion thanks to its lightweight construction, accessibility to maps and navigation apps, language translation capabilities, and entertainment alternatives. Additionally, its lengthy battery life guarantees that users may remain amused and connected while traveling.

- **Freelancers**: The adaptability of the iPad is advantageous to freelancers in a variety of fields, including authors, graphic designers, photographers, and consultants. It gives users the freedom to handle projects remotely, interact with clients, and present their portfolios.

- **Real estate**: Real estate agents use the iPad to manage client databases, offer virtual tours, and present property listings with rich multimedia material. It is a useful tool for property presentations and client contacts due to its mobility and simplicity of usage.
- **Sales and Marketing**: The iPad can be a valuable tool for sales and marketing professionals. They can use it to make an impression during presentations, access sales materials, maintain contact with customers, and monitor sales progress while they are on the go.
- **Seniors and Elderly**: The iPad is a great device for the elderly, thanks to its user-friendly UI and accessibility capabilities. It provides a simple user interface for keeping in touch with loved ones via video conversations, accessing helpful health monitoring apps, and taking part in hobbies or learning new skills.

These are just a few illustrations of the various user types that the iPad can help. Its potential for different user demographics will grow as the gadget develops and new apps are created, making it a vital tool in many facets of our lives.

WHICH IPAD MODEL IS BEST FOR YOU?

What Specifications and Features to Look Out for When Choosing an iPad

Choosing the right iPad involves considering various specifications and features that directly impact the user experience and performance. This section will go through the important factors to consider when choosing an iPad and their importance. Additionally, we will provide step-by-step guides on how to access and enable certain features.

Screen Size: The iPad's display's physical dimensions are determined by the screen size. It normally ranges from 7.9 inches (iPad mini) to 12.9 inches (iPad Pro) when measured diagonally. When watching movies, editing images, or working on creative projects, a larger screen size delivers a more immersive viewing experience. You can check the product description on websites run by authorized resellers or go to the official Apple website to examine the screen size specifications for each iPad model.

Screen Resolution: The number of pixels displayed on the screen, which determines the degree of clarity and sharpness, is referred to as screen resolution. Crisper images and finer details are produced by higher resolution. The iPad's Retina display, which offers exceptional image quality and brilliant colors, is the resolution that is most frequently used. Go to Settings > Display & Brightness > Display Resolution on an iPad to access and view the screen resolution.

Battery Life: The iPad's battery life indicates how long it can operate without requiring recharging. It is a crucial factor to take into account, particularly for customers who need prolonged usage but do not have access to a power source. The battery life of different iPad models varies, with newer models typically offering longer usage hours. Visit the official Apple website or authorized reseller websites to view battery life details for various iPad models.

Processor: The iPad's processor, also known as the CPU (Central Processing Unit), controls the device's speed and general performance. iPads are powered by Apple's A-series CPUs, and each new generation offers higher speed, enabling quicker app loading, more fluid multitasking, and better graphics. Visit the official Apple website or look at websites for accredited resellers to learn more about the processing specifications for each iPad model.

Storage: The amount of data that can be kept on the iPad, including apps, pictures, videos, and documents, is determined by the storage capacity. Storage capacities range from 32GB to 1TB or more, depending on the device. It's crucial to take into account your storage requirements based on how the device will be used. Visit the official Apple website or a website run by a licensed reseller to explore the available storage options and select the right size.

Front and rear cameras: iPads have front and rear cameras that can be used for document scanning, making video calls, and taking pictures and movies. The camera's specifications cover its megapixel count, aperture size, and extras like HDR (High Dynamic Range) and picture stabilization. Better image quality is achieved by using cameras with more megapixels and sophisticated functions. Locate the Camera app on the home screen of an iPad to access and utilize the camera. Then, adhere to the on-screen directions to take pictures or movies.

Size and Weight: An iPad's portability and usability are impacted by its physical size and weight. Users that prioritize mobility will find lighter, more compact devices convenient, while larger, heavier models frequently have more sophisticated capabilities. Visit the official Apple website or look at the websites of accredited resellers to view the dimensions and weight of a particular iPad model.

Operating System: The iPad's operating system (OS) controls its functionality, interface, and app compatibility. Apple updates its operating system frequently, adding improvements, security patches, and fresh features. If you want to use the most recent features and functionalities, make sure your chosen iPad model is compatible with the most recent OS release. Go to the official Apple website or the iPad's Settings > General > Software Update to see if an iPad is compatible with the most recent operating system.

Connectivity: Wi-Fi and cellular data are among the connectivity choices available on iPads. Cellular data offers internet access over a mobile network, but Wi-Fi permits access to the internet when linked to a wireless network. Additionally, cellular models demand a unique data plan from a service provider. Go to Settings > Wi-Fi or Settings > Cellular Data on the iPad to view and modify the Wi-Fi or cellular data settings.

Compatibility with Other Apple Devices: Apple products are made to operate in harmony with one another. The seamless integration and data sharing between iPads and other Apple products, including iPhones, Macs, and Apple Watches, is made possible by their compatibility. This compatibility can increase convenience and productivity. Consult the official Apple website or authorized reseller websites for compatibility information to ensure compatibility with other Apple devices.

Unique Features: Depending on the generation, each iPad model may include special features. Support for the Apple Pencil, Face ID or Touch ID biometric verification, ProMotion technology for responsiveness and smooth scrolling, and improved audio capabilities are a few examples of these features. Visit the official Apple website to learn more about the distinctive characteristics of each iPad model, or consult the websites of accredited resellers for complete details.

By considering these details and characteristics, you may select the iPad model that best meets your requirements and preferences. Always consult the official

Apple website or the websites of accredited resellers for detailed specifications and step-by-step instructions on how to access and enable particular functionalities.

What Are the Different iPad Models?

To meet the needs of diverse users, the iPad series offers a variety of models. Let's examine the many iPad versions now on the market, their main characteristics, technical details, and applicability to various customers.

A powerful A12Z Bionic chip, Face ID, and an edge-to-edge Liquid Retina XDR display are all included in the 12.9-inch iPad Pro (6th Generation). It features USB-C connectivity, up to 2TB of storage, second-generation Apple Pencil support, and Magic Keyboard compatibility. Professionals and power users that require a huge canvas and exceptional performance should choose this model.

The A12Z Bionic CPU, Face ID, and brilliant Liquid Retina display come standard on the 11-inch iPad Pro (4th Generation). It offers USB-C connectivity, up to 1TB of storage, second-generation Apple Pencil functionality, and Magic Keyboard compatibility. Professionals, students, and creatives can all use this model because it is powerful and portable.

A 10.9-inch Liquid Retina display, Touch ID, and the potent A14 Bionic CPU are all included in the iPad Air (5th Generation). It features USB-C connectivity, up to 256GB of storage, second-generation Apple Pencil functionality, and Magic Keyboard compatibility. Students, professionals, and casual users looking for a balance between portability and performance may consider the iPad Air.

The 10.2-inch Retina display, Touch ID, and A13 Bionic CPU are all features of the iPad (9th Generation). It has a Lightning connector, up to 256GB of storage, and first-generation Apple Pencil and Smart Keyboard compatibility. This option is affordable for all users, including families, students, and casual users.

There are features shared by both the 9th and 10th generations of iPads. An economical and adaptable iPad is perfect for families, students, and casual users.

Touch ID, the potent A15 Bionic CPU, and an 8.3-inch Liquid Retina display are all features of the iPad mini (6th Generation). It features USB-C connectivity, up to 256GB of storage, and second-generation Apple Pencil functionality. Users who prefer portability and want a smaller iPad might choose the iPad mini.

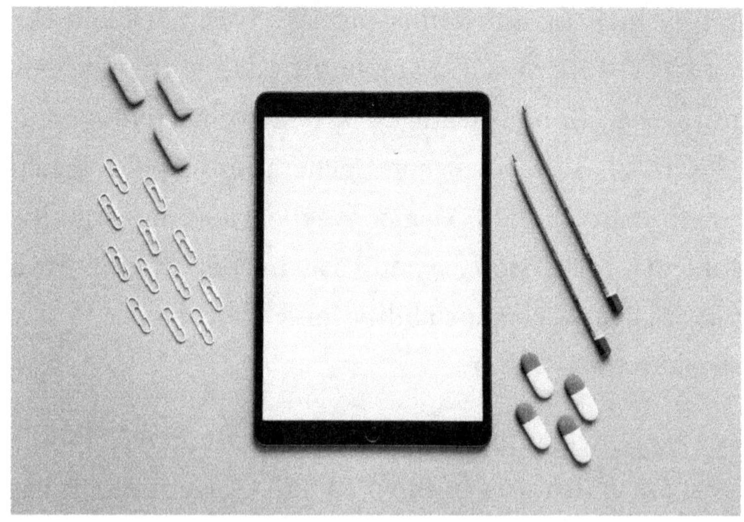

SEGUE

This chapter covered the definition of an iPad, its key features, specifications to take into account when making a choice, and how different iPad models vary in terms of their usefulness for diverse users. Each iPad model—including the 12.9-inch and 11-inch iPad Pro models—as well as the iPad Air, normal iPad models, and iPad mini—is designed to meet a particular purpose, whether it be for businesspeople, students, casual users, or people looking for portability. With this knowledge, readers may securely select the right iPad model to meet their needs. We'll move our attention to senior-friendly iPad features in the chapter after that, which will improve usability and accessibility for senior users. By offering information about senior-friendly options, we hope to improve the iPad experience for all users, regardless of their age or level of technological expertise.

2

SENIOR-FRIENDLY OPTIONS ON THE IPAD

It is essential for mobile device designers and developers to take into account the needs of various age groups, especially the elderly, in today's technologically advanced society. With its iPad devices, Apple, a pioneer in innovation, has made great strides toward designing inclusive and approachable user experiences. The text size, voice control, and accessibility options for people with vision, hearing, and movement limitations are just a few of the features and settings that may be changed to make the iPad user-friendly for seniors. Readers will be equipped with the knowledge and expertise necessary to customize the iPad for elders by the end of this chapter, providing a fun and welcoming digital experience. Let's work together to provide seniors with the confidence and comfort they need to embrace the digital world.

HOW TO MAKE THE IPAD EASIER TO USE FOR SENIORS

It is essential to make sure that everyone, especially seniors and the elderly, can use and benefit from modern electronics as they become more and more integrated into our daily lives. The iPad provides seniors with a multitude of chances to stay connected, engaged, and informed thanks to its user-friendly UI and configurable capabilities. This comprehensive guide will examine the many iPad accessibility settings that can be modified to accommodate the particular requirements of senior users. Seniors can improve their iPad experience and easily utilize its features by enabling and adjusting these settings.

Accessing Accessibility Settings

Before delving into specific accessibility features, it's important to know how to access the accessibility settings on the iPad. Here's a step-by-step guide to help readers find and navigate these settings:

1. Open the "Settings" app on the iPad.
2. Tap on "Accessibility" in the left-hand menu.

3. A list of accessibility features and settings will appear, allowing you to customize your iPad experience according to your preferences and needs.

Exploring Accessibility Settings

Zoom and Magnify

Zoom and Magnify are invaluable tools for seniors with visual impairments. They allow users to enlarge the screen content for easier readability. Here's how to enable and customize Zoom and Magnify:

1. Access the Accessibility settings as described earlier.
2. Tap on "Zoom" and toggle the switch to enable it.
3. To obtain a suitable magnification level, use the slider to adjust the Zoom level.
4. To magnify specific areas, enable the "Follow Focus" and "Show Controller" options.

Increase or Reduce the Contrast

Changing the contrast can make text easier to see and reduce strain on the eyes. Seniors can customize the contrast settings on their iPads using the following steps:

1. Go to Accessibility Settings.
2. Tap on "Display & Text Size."
3. Toggle on "Increase Contrast" to adjust the appearance of buttons, icons, and other interface elements.
4. By turning on the "Reduce Transparency" option, transparency will be reduced.

Voice Commands

For seniors with limited mobility, voice commands offer an alternative way to control the iPad. The built-in Siri feature allows users to interact with the device using their voice. To set up and utilize voice commands:

1. Open "Settings" and go to "Accessibility."
2. Tap on "Voice Control" and toggle it on.
3. To configure voice commands, adhere to the on-screen directions.
4. You can use various voice commands to navigate, open apps, send messages, and perform other tasks.

Customizing Font Style and Size

Customizing font style and size can significantly improve readability for seniors. To make adjustments:

1. Access the "Display & Text Size" section in Accessibility settings.
2. Tap on "Larger Text" to enable larger font sizes.
3. Drag the slider to choose the desired font size, or select "Customize Size" for finer adjustments.
4. To change the font style, tap on "Bold Text" or "Button Shapes" for clearer text and interface elements.

Changing App Sizes

Some seniors may find it challenging to interact with smaller app icons or text. The iPad allows users to resize app icons and text to enhance visibility. Here's how:

1. Navigate to Accessibility Settings.
2. Tap on "Display & Text Size."
3. Choosing "App Icon Size" will allow you to change the size of the app icons on your home screen.
4. To change the text size within apps, enable "Larger Text" and adjust the slider as desired.

Reducing Transparency

Reducing transparency can make the user interface more distinct and easier to read. Follow these steps:

1. Accessibility settings.
2. Tap on "Display & Text Size."
3. Enable "Reduce Transparency" to reduce the visual transparency effects throughout the interface.

AssistiveTouch

AssistiveTouch offers an on-screen virtual menu that allows users to access essential functions without physically pressing buttons. To enable AssistiveTouch:

1. Go to Accessibility Settings.
2. Tap on "Touch."
3. Select "AssistiveTouch" and toggle it on.
4. Customize the virtual menu by selecting "Customize Top Level Menu" and adding desired actions.

Touch Accommodation

Touch Accommodation is designed to help users with motor skill challenges by adjusting touch sensitivity. To set up Touch Accommodation,

1. Accessibility settings.
2. Tap on "Touch."
3. Enable "Touch Accommodations."
4. Adjust the "Hold Duration" and "Ignore Repeat" settings according to your needs.

Guided Access

Guided Access locks the iPad to a specific app, preventing accidental exits or unauthorized access. Navigate to the accessibility settings to enable guided access.

1. Select "Guided Access" from the "Learning" menu by tapping it.
2. Put a passcode in place and turn "Guided Access" on.
3. To enable Guided Access, open the relevant app, triple-click the home button (or side button, depending on the iPad model), and choose "Start."

Subtitles and Captioning

For seniors with hearing impairments, enabling subtitles and captioning enhances their multimedia experience. Here's how:

1. Accessibility settings.
2. Tap on "Subtitles & Captioning."
3. Toggle on "Closed Captions + SDH" for built-in captions or "Subtitles & Captioning Style" for customizable options.
4. To suit your preferences, change the parameters for the text size, color, and backdrop.

For seniors and the elderly, the iPad's configurable accessibility settings can greatly improve their user experience. Older users can comfortably use and engage with their iPads by activating and modifying features like Zoom and Magnify, contrast adjustments, voice commands, font customization, and more. This detailed guide seeks to enable seniors and the people who care for them to utilize these capabilities to the fullest extent possible, ensuring that technology is usable and enjoyed by people of all ages.

THE BEST APPS AND ACCESSORIES FOR SENIORS

Apps offer a vast range of functionality and entertainment possibilities, and they have become a crucial part of our daily lives in the digital age. The use of apps by seniors can significantly improve their iPad experience, offering convenience, enjoyment, and chances to improve their health and well-being. This post will showcase several apps from a variety of categories, such as entertainment, utility, and health, and will include details on their functions as well as instructions on how to download, install, and use them successfully.

Entertainment Apps

Entertainment apps offer seniors a diverse range of activities, from games and puzzles to reading and music. These apps promote cognitive stimulation, creativity, and relaxation.

Sudoku

Sudoku is a popular number puzzle game that enhances logical thinking and problem-solving skills. accessible through the App Store

- Install and Download: In the App Store, type "Sudoku" and select "Install" to download and set up the application.
- How to Use: Select a difficulty level, tap on the grid, and input numbers to complete the puzzle.

Kindle

Kindle allows seniors to access a vast library of ebooks and enjoy reading on their iPad. Accessible through the App Store

- Search for "Kindle" in the App Store and select "Install" to download and install the application.
- How to Use: Sign in with an Amazon account, browse or search for books, select a book to read, and customize reading settings for personalized preferences.

Convenience Apps

Convenience apps aim to simplify daily tasks, provide information, and enhance communication, making life easier for seniors.

Zoom

Zoom is a video conferencing app that enables seniors to connect with family and friends through video calls accessible through the App Store

- Install and Download: In the App Store, type "Zoom" and select "Install" to download and set up the application.

- How to Use: Create an account or join a
  meeting using the provided meeting ID and
  password, adjust video and audio settings, and
  initiate or join video calls with contacts.

Google Maps

Google Maps offers seniors reliable navigation, directions, and information about local businesses and services. Accessible through the App Store

- Install and Download: In the App Store, look
  for "Google Maps" and select "Install" to
  download and install the program.

- How to Use: Launch the app, enter the desired destination, view routes, and receive step-by-step directions with voice guidance.

Health Apps

Health apps cater to seniors' well-being, promoting fitness, medication management, and overall health monitoring.

MyFitnessPal

MyFitnessPal is a comprehensive app that tracks nutrition, calories, exercise, and weight management. Accessible through the App Store

- Install and Download: In the App Store, look for "MyFitnessPal" and select "Install" to download and set up the program.
- How to Use: Create an account, set health goals, log food and exercise, and track progress towards maintaining a healthy lifestyle.

Medisafe

Medisafe helps seniors manage their medications by providing reminders, refill alerts, and tracking features. Accessible through the App Store

- Install and Download: In the App Store, type "Medisafe" and select "Install" to download and set up the application.
- How to Use: Set up medication reminders, input medication details, receive notifications for doses, and track adherence to medication schedules.

Accepting the world of applications can significantly improve seniors' iPad experiences by offering enjoyment, convenience, and better health. These apps meet the varied demands of senior users, whether it be through entertaining games like Sudoku, easy access to a huge library with Kindle, streamlining work with Zoom and Google Maps, or encouraging fitness and medication management with MyFitnessPal and Medisafe.

Accessories

The ideal accessories can significantly improve the usability and convenience of iPads for seniors. These attachments cater to the particular needs and preferences of elderly users while also adding functionality. This section will highlight a variety of iPad accessories that can make for a better user experience for elders. We'll go through each accessory's function, where to acquire it, and how to integrate and utilize it with the iPad.

Cases

Cases serve as protective covers for iPads, safeguarding them from accidental bumps, scratches, and falls. They also offer additional features to enhance usability. Cases protect the iPad from damage and provide added functionality, such as built-in stands for hands-free viewing or adjustable angles for comfortable typing.

- Where to Buy: Numerous vendors, both online and offline, provide cases for sale. Websites like Amazon, Best Buy, and Apple's official website offer a wide selection of iPad cases.
- How to Use/Integrate: Simply slide the iPad into the case, ensuring a secure fit. Depending on the case, it may feature a stand or adjustable angles that allow users to prop up the iPad for optimal viewing or typing positions.

Stylus

A stylus is a pen-like device that allows users to interact with the iPad's touchscreen more accurately and comfortably, providing precise control.

- Purpose: Styluses provide a more precise and comfortable input method for older users, especially those with dexterity or mobility issues. They enhance accuracy when tapping icons, typing, drawing, or navigating the iPad.
- Where to Buy: Styluses are widely available, and options can be found on websites like Amazon, Best Buy, and Apple's official website.
- How to Use/Integrate: Simply hold the stylus like a pen and use it to interact with the iPad's touch screen. It offers better precision and control compared to using fingers, making it easier for seniors to navigate through apps, input text, and perform other tasks.

Power Cables

Power cables are essential accessories that ensure the iPad remains charged and ready for use. Power cables provide a reliable source of power to charge the iPad's battery, ensuring uninterrupted usage.

- Where to Buy: Power cables can be purchased from Apple's official website, authorized resellers, or reputable electronics retailers.
- How to Use/Integrate: One end of the power cord should be connected to the iPad's charging port, and the other end should be connected to

a power source such as a wall adapter or a USB connection on a computer. Charging can take place while the iPad is in use or when it is not in use.

Headphones

Headphones are audio accessories that enable seniors to enjoy immersive and personalized audio experiences on their iPads. Headphones allow users to listen to music, watch videos, participate in video calls, or access audio content without disturbing others. They provide better sound quality and can help seniors with hearing difficulties hear more clearly.

- Where to Buy: Headphones can be purchased from various retailers, including electronics stores, online marketplaces like Amazon, and Apple's official website.
- How to Use/Integrate: Connect the headphones to the iPad's audio jack or use wireless headphones that connect via Bluetooth. Seniors can adjust the volume and use any accompanying controls on the headphones to manage audio playback.

SEGUE

This chapter focuses on making the iPad more accessible and user-friendly for seniors. We talked about modifying settings for people with visual, hearing, and mobility disabilities, such as text size, voice control, and accessibility features. In order to improve their everyday tasks and internet experience, we also looked into assistive technology and apps designed specifically for seniors. For improved usability, recommended accessories like cases and styluses were given. We'll give data security and privacy top priority in the following chapter. We'll talk about important security methods like data encryption, biometrics, and passcodes. We'll place a focus on backup tools, safe browsing, and managing app permissions in order to give you peace of mind.

3

PROTECT YOUR IPAD DATA— IMPORTANT SECURITY AND DATA PRIVACY TIPS

We'll examine important security and data privacy aspects of iPads in this chapter to protect your private data. In the era of privacy invasions and data breaches we live in today, protecting the data on your iPad is essential. You may establish a safe digital area for personal and professional use by adjusting auto-lock settings, turning on Face ID or Touch ID, and setting strong passcodes. Discover two-factor authentication and Find My iPad to stop unauthorized access and locate your tablet in case it is misplaced. Data privacy will be improved by updating apps often, controlling permissions, and utilizing secure networks. You can secure your cloud data by using two-factor authentication and strong passwords.

IMPORTANT SECURITY SETTINGS TO ENABLE ON YOUR DEVICE

Security is of utmost importance in the modern digital era, especially when it comes to our own devices like iPads. Your data will stay secure and confidential from potential dangers if the appropriate security settings are enabled. In this thorough guide, we'll take you step-by-step through the process of accessing and configuring crucial security features on your iPad, including securing online browsing, using Lockdown Mode, managing app permissions and privacy settings, and preventing access.

Protecting Access to Your iPad

Passcode: A basic security measure that guards against unauthorized access to your iPad is the passcode. The steps below can be used to create a passcode:

1. Open "Settings" on your iPad in step one.
2. Depending on your iPad model, tap "Touch ID & Passcode" or "Face ID & Passcode."
3. If the option "Turn Passcode On" is not already selected, select it.
4. Type in the passcode you choose (at least six digits are advised).
5. Verify the passcode to activate it.

Touch/Face ID: If your iPad has Touch ID (fingerprint recognition) or Face ID (facial recognition) capabilities, you might want to turn these features on for more security and convenience. These procedures should be followed to set up Touch ID or Face ID: Open "Settings" on your iPad in step one.

1. Select either "Touch ID & Passcode" or "Face ID & Passcode."
2. Adhere to the on-screen directions to configure Touch ID or Face ID.

Auto-lock: After a predetermined amount of inactivity, auto-lock secures your iPad, making sure it is never left unprotected and exposed. Activate auto-lock by performing the following:

1. Open "Settings" on your iPad in step one.
2. Then, select "Display & Brightness."
3. Choose the auto-lock time you want (for instance, 2 minutes).

Lost Device Protection and Find My iPad: Find My iPad is an invaluable feature that helps you locate your lost or stolen device. To enable it, follow these steps:

1. Open "Settings" on your iPad in step one.

2. Tap the top-right Apple ID button.
3. Decide on "Find My."
4. Activate "Find My iPad" and "Send Last Location."

Controlling What Features Are Available Without Unlocking Your iPad

Limiting access to certain features when your iPad is locked enhances security. To control this, follow these steps:

1. Open "Settings" on your iPad in step one.
2. a. Select either "Touch ID & Passcode" or "Face ID & Passcode."
3. c. Select which functions to activate or disable under "Allow Access When Locked," such as Today View, Notification Center, and Control Center.

What to Do If You Forgot Your Passcode: In case you forget your passcode, you can regain access to your iPad by following these steps:

1. Connect your iPad to a machine running iTunes.
2. Restart your iPad forcibly (various techniques apply depending on the model of iPad; see the linked links for more information).

3. Use iTunes' on-screen prompts to restore your iPad and set it up from a backup or as new.

App Permissions and Privacy

App Tracking: iOS introduces App Tracking Transparency, allowing users to control which apps can track their data across other apps and websites. To manage app tracking, follow these steps:

1. Open "Settings" on your iPad in step one.
2. Toggle "Privacy."
3. Decide on "Tracking."
4. To enable or disable app tracking, turn the switches next to each app on or off.

App Permissions: When installing new apps, you'll be prompted to grant specific permissions. To manage these permissions later, follow these steps:

1. Open "Settings" on your iPad in step one.
2. Toggle "Privacy."
3. Look over the different categories (such as Camera, Microphone, and Location Services) and decide which apps are allowed access to these features.

Privacy Settings and Web Browsing

Making Account Sign-ins Safer and Easier:

1. Start your iPad's "Settings" app.
2. Select "Passwords."
3. Turn on "AutoFill Passwords" to allow Safari to safely store and fill in your passwords.

Data Cache and Cookies:

1. Start your iPad's "Settings" app.
2. Select "Safari."
3. Select "Clear History and Website Data" to delete cookies and browsing history from websites.

Email Privacy:

For email privacy, use strong passwords and consider enabling two-factor authentication (2FA) where available. Be cautious of suspicious email links and attachments to avoid phishing attempts.

Lockdown Mode

Lockdown Mode is an additional security measure designed to protect your iPad in specific situations, such as protests or encounters with law enforcement.

When activated, it restricts access to your device, preventing anyone from forcing you to unlock it without your consent. To enable Lockdown Mode, follow these steps:

1. Open the **Settings** app.
2. Tap **Privacy & Security**.
3. Under **Security**, tap **Lockdown Mode**.
4. Tap **Turn On Lockdown Mode**.
5. Tap **Turn On and Restart**.
6. Enter your device's passcode.

To safeguard your private information and preserve your privacy, safeguarding your iPad should be a top priority. You may benefit from a safer and more secure online experience by turning on these crucial security options. To protect your important data and feel at ease in a constantly connected environment, be alert, keep your iPad updated, and use these features.

PRIVACY IN THE CLOUD: ICLOUD SETTINGS AND DATA STORAGE

The cloud-based iCloud service from Apple lets customers save and synchronize their data across various devices. It safely saves and provides easy access to images, videos, documents, contacts, calendar events, app data, and more from any Apple device logged in with the same Apple ID. We will cover crucial privacy issues in this part while utilizing iCloud to protect your iPad's data on the cloud.

A Step-by-Step Guide to Secure Your iPad Data in the Cloud

Securing your Apple ID: Your Apple ID is the key to accessing iCloud and all of Apple's services. Protecting it is crucial to preventing unauthorized access to your account and data.

1. Make a secure password: Choose a password for your Apple ID that is unique and difficult, using a combination of upper- and lower-case letters, digits, and special characters.
2. Turn on Two-Factor Authentication (2FA): When you sign in with your Apple ID, 2FA adds an extra degree of security by requiring a verification code sent to your trusted devices or phone number. Go to Settings > [your name] > Password & Security > Two-Factor Authentication to enable it.
3. Examine Trusted Devices: Examine the list of trusted devices associated with your Apple ID on a regular basis. To protect account security,

delete any devices you no longer use or recognize.

4. Using iCloud Private Relay: iCloud Private Relay is a privacy feature available with iCloud+ that improves the security and privacy of internet browsing. It conceals your IP address and encrypts your internet data, making third-party tracking of your online activities more difficult.

5. Turn on iCloud Private Relay: Go to Settings > [your name] > iCloud > Private Relay to enable iCloud Private Relay. Turn on "iCloud Private Relay" to enable this feature.

Backing up your data in the Cloud: Backing up your iPad data to iCloud is essential to protect against data loss due to device damage, theft, or other unforeseen events.

1. Enabling iCloud Backup: is as simple as going to Settings > [your name] > iCloud > iCloud Backup. Toggle "iCloud Backup" on or off to allow automatic backups.

2. Manual Backup: At any moment, you can perform a manual backup by navigating to Settings > [your name] > iCloud > iCloud Backup > Back Up Now.

3. Check the Backup Status: Check the "Last Backup" time under iCloud Backup to ensure your data is routinely backed up. The most recent backup date and time should be displayed here.

4. Manage Backup Data: Go to Settings > [your name] > iCloud > Manage Storage > Backups > [your device name] to select which apps' data to backup. You can turn off apps that you don't want to backup here.

What to do if you forget your Apple ID password

If you forget your Apple ID password, you can reset it to regain access to your account and data.

Make use of the Apple ID Account Page: Click "Forgot Apple ID or Password?" on the Apple ID account page. To reset your password, follow the on-screen instructions.

Use Your Trusted Device: If you've enabled 2FA, you can reset your password using your trusted device. Follow the steps to go to Settings > [your name] > Password & Security > Change Password.

Use Account Recovery: If you don't have access to your trusted device, you can use account recovery on the password reset page by selecting "Don't have access to any of your devices?" To finish the account recovery process, follow the instructions.

By carefully following the procedures described here, you can ensure the protection of your iPad data stored in the cloud via iCloud. Your data will be safer if you protect your Apple ID, enable iCloud Private Relay, and back it up frequently. If you forget your Apple ID password, knowing the recovery steps might help you regain access to your account and appropriately protect your data.

PROTECTING YOUR IPAD AGAINST ONLINE THREATS

Strong security measures and iOS, Apple's mobile operating system, are well-known for being found on iPads. Although it is true that iPads are less prone to conventional viruses than other platforms, they are not completely impervious to all online dangers. Cyberthreats are evolving along with technology; therefore, it is crucial for iPad users to be cautious and take the necessary precautions to secure their data. This detailed tutorial will cover a variety of online issues that may impact iPads as well as offer helpful advice on how to protect your iPad from them.

Understanding Digital Attacks

Virus

A virus is a malicious software program that attaches itself to legitimate files and spreads from one device to another. Although iPads are unlikely to be infected by traditional computer viruses due to the iOS sandboxing architecture, it's essential to remain cautious while downloading and installing apps from untrusted sources.

Prevention: Stick to the official App Store for app downloads because Apple meticulously reviews and vets all programs to guarantee they satisfy security standards.

If Affected: If you encounter unusual behavior on your iPad or suspect a virus, remove any suspicious apps and run a thorough scan using reputable antivirus software for iOS.

Malware

Malware, short for malicious software, is a broad term that includes a variety of dangers, such as spyware, adware, and ransomware. These programs can be concealed within seemingly harmless apps, email attachments, or websites.

Prevention: Avoid downloading software from unknown sites, be wary of email attachments, and avoid clicking on strange URLs.

If affected, immediately uninstall any suspicious apps and run an antivirus scan. Consider resetting your iPad to factory settings if the malware persists.

Ransomware

Ransomware is a sort of software that encrypts your files and requires a ransom to be paid in order to decrypt them. While less prevalent on iOS, it is not entirely unheard of.

Prevention: Regularly back up your data to iCloud or an external device to minimize the impact of a potential ransomware attack.

If affected, Do not pay the ransom, as there's no guarantee the attackers will provide the decryption key. Restore your iPad from an earlier backup instead.

Adware

Adware displays unwanted advertisements, pop-ups, and banners, often affecting the device's performance and user experience.

Prevention: Avoid downloading apps from untrusted sources and be selective about the permissions you grant to applications.

If affected, remove any suspicious apps causing adware and consider installing an ad blocker from the App Store.

Spyware

Spyware secretly gathers information about your device and activities without your knowledge, posing a significant privacy risk.

Prevention: Be cautious while granting permissions to apps and review app privacy settings regularly.

If affected, remove any suspicious apps and consider using an antivirus app to detect and eliminate spyware.

Attempts to Breach Private Data

Scams

Scams come in various forms, such as fake lottery winnings, tech support scams, or offers that are too good to be true. These frauds try to lure consumers into disclosing private information or sending money to phony accounts.

Prevention: Be wary of unsolicited mail, stay away from dubious sites, and don't provide private information.

If Affected: If you suspect you've fallen for a scam, contact your bank immediately to block any fraudulent transactions and report the incident to the relevant authorities.

Phishing

Phishing attempts deceive consumers into supplying sensitive information like login credentials or credit card details by using fake emails, messages, or websites.

Prevention: Be skeptical of unsolicited requests for personal information and verify the sender's identity before sharing any sensitive data.

If Affected: Change your passwords right away and enable two-factor authentication for additional security if you believe you've been the victim of a phishing scam.

Hacking

Hacking involves unauthorized access to your device or accounts, potentially leading to data theft or privacy breaches.

Prevention: Use strong, unique passwords for your accounts, enable two-factor authentication, and keep your iPad's software updated.

If affected: If you suspect unauthorized access to your iPad, change your Apple ID password immediately and contact Apple Support for assistance.

Spoofing

Spoofing involves impersonating legitimate entities like websites or email addresses to deceive users into trusting fraudulent sources.

Prevention: Before sending any sensitive data, be sure that websites and emails are legitimate.

If affected, Report the spoofing incident to the relevant authorities and avoid engaging further with the spoofed entity.

SEGUE

This chapter focuses on the importance of safeguarding iPad data from various internet dangers, including viruses and phishing. There are comprehensive instructions for safeguarding the iPad, including how to activate two-factor authentication and use iCloud Private Relay. To avoid fraud and hacking attempts, users are recommended to use strong passwords, exercise care, and confirm the sender's identity. A safe digital experience requires being aware and taking preventive measures, despite strong security measures. The following chapter will examine a variety of crucial add-ons to improve the iPad user experience while balancing security and usefulness for peak performance.

4

MUST-HAVE IPAD ACCESSORIES FOR EVERY USER

In this chapter, learn about the variety of stylish and useful accessories that other users have adorned their iPads with. These accessories not only improve the look of the gadget but also provide crucial convenience and security. Discover a selection of necessary iPad accessories created to satisfy every user's needs. Learn about the advantages they offer in terms of function and aesthetics to protect and enhance your iPad experience. These accessories go beyond aesthetics, enhancing comfort and productivity. They range from sturdy phone covers that protect against spills and bumps to screen protectors for a spotless display. Find the ideal accessories to improve the use and style of your iPad, whether you're a professional or a student.

THE ULTIMATE LIST OF ACCESSORIES EVERY IPAD OWNER MUST HAVE

The opportunities for productivity, pleasure, and creativity are boundless when you own an iPad. Having the proper accessories for your iPad is crucial for maximizing its potential. We'll go through a long list of essential accessories in this guide, such as cases and covers, keyboards and mice, headphones and speakers, chargers and cables, and other accessories like screen protectors, external drives/SSDs, flash drives, multi-port adapters. Each item will be thoroughly described, including its application, advantages for particular user types, pertinent key points, characteristics to consider, advantages and disadvantages, suggested brands, typical market prices, and where to buy information.

Cases and Covers

Protective Cases

All users of your iPad will benefit from the security and increased longevity that protective covers offer. By protecting your iPad from bumps, drops, and dings, these covers give it an extra degree of security. To protect your iPad from potential harm, use impact-resistant materials like polycarbonate or shock-absorbing TPU. For uninterrupted functionality, precise cutouts are essential since they make it simple to reach all connections, buttons, and camera lenses. The performance of the gadget shouldn't be hampered by a well-made cover.

Numerous choices are available from reputable manufacturers, such as Apple Smart Cover/Smart Folio, Speck, and OtterBox. OtterBox excels at producing tough cases for challenging environments, while Speck provides elegant and fashionable options. The iPad's thin profile is maintained by Apple's Smart Cover/Smart Folio; however, it offers very little screen protection.

The price of protective coverings ranges from $30 to $100, depending on the manufacturer, the materials, and any other features. There are solutions that are affordable without sacrificing quality, and more expensive products could be necessary for certain features. There is a large assortment to suit tastes and budgets at Apple's approved retail locations and online retailers like Amazon.

Keyboard Cases

Professionals, students, and content creators using iPads now enjoy unprecedented productivity and freedom thanks to keyboard cases. These covers turn iPads into laptop-like devices, enhancing the typing experience and making it possible to perform things like writing, editing, and document creation. Features like backlit keys for convenient typing in low light or when traveling should be taken into account when selecting a keyboard case. When necessary, detachable keyboards enable seamless transitions between tablet and laptop modes. For prolonged productivity when working or studying, a long battery life is essential.

For various iPad versions, reputable manufacturers like Logitech, Brydge, and Apple Smart Keyboard Folio offer premium keyboard cases. Prices range from $80 to $200, and more expensive cases can offer a more comfortable typing experience. A large variety of keyboard cases are available from official websites and electronics stores to meet different tastes and price ranges, enhancing the usability and efficiency of the iPad for consumers.

Keyboards and Mice

Bluetooth Keyboards

Bluetooth keyboards are a great choice for iPad owners looking for a comfortable typing experience during extended sessions. The ability to position the keyboard wherever with respect to the iPad without cords makes these compact and lightweight keyboards ideal for writing, taking notes, and text-intensive activities. Multi-device connectivity, which enables easy switching between the iPad, smartphone, and PC for a variety of applications, is an essential aspect to take into account.

In order to ensure continuous use without regular recharging, Bluetooth keyboards have long-lasting batteries. They work more effectively when equipped with battery-saving features like automatic sleep mode while inactive. A variety of Bluetooth keyboards are available at various price points from reputable manufacturers, including Logitech, Anker, and the Microsoft Surface Keyboard. Anker offers inexpensive, compact designs with outstanding battery life, while Logitech specializes in making strong, ergonomic keyboards for a great typing experience. Aesthetics and functionality lovers will appreciate the chic Microsoft Surface Keyboard.

Bluetooth keyboards range in price from $30 to $100, with the more expensive ones coming with extras like lighted keys and sturdy construction. The official websites of Microsoft, Anker, and Logitech are trustworthy sources for in-depth product information and customer support. As an alternative, well-known electronics retailers and online markets like Amazon provide a wide selection of Bluetooth keyboards to suit different tastes and price ranges.

Bluetooth Mice

Bluetooth mice provide a wireless option that improves productivity and navigation for graphic artists and painters seeking fine cursor control. They are perfect for intricate editing and sophisticated design work due to their quick cursor reaction. Adjustable DPI, which enables users to tailor cursor sensitivity to their preferences and accommodates a variety of creative jobs, is a crucial feature to take into account.

Ergonomic design is also essential to guarantee comfort throughout extended use without hand fatigue. For improved ergonomics, certain models have rubber grips and curved curves. A range of Bluetooth mice are available from reputable manufacturers like Logitech, Microsoft, and Apple Magic Mouse that are tailored to varied tastes and hand sizes. Microsoft offers fashionable, smooth-tracking ergonomic mice designed for creative professionals, while Logitech stands out for its trustworthy and feature-rich offerings. The Magic Mouse from Apple is especially made for Apple gadgets, guaranteeing a perfect fit and compatibility.

Prices for Bluetooth mice range from $20 to $100, with more expensive ones offering programmable buttons and better tracking features. On the official websites of these businesses, you may find thorough product information and customer service to help you make an informed purchase. Customers can find the ideal match for their interests and budget thanks to the variety of options offered by electronics retailers and online marketplaces like Amazon.

Headphones and Speakers

Noise-Canceling Headphones

For regular travelers and audiophiles seeking an immersive listening experience, noise-canceling headphones are a game-changer. These cutting-edge headphones are made to suppress outside noise, resulting in a peaceful and quiet soundscape. Noise-canceling headphones enable you to block out distractions and fully engross yourself in your preferred music, podcasts, or audiobooks, whether you're in a crowded cafe or a noisy airplane.

When selecting noise-canceling headphones, it's crucial to seek out premium brands that lead the pack in this technology. The noise-canceling headphones offered by Sony, a pioneer in audio innovation, are renowned for their excellent sound quality and efficient noise cancellation. Another well-known brand is Bose, which is recognized for its noise-canceling technology, which offers a serene listening experience even in busy settings. The Apple AirPods Pro have active noise suppression and transparency mode for a personalized experience, and they seamlessly integrate with Apple devices.

Depending on the brand, sound quality, and other features, noise-canceling headphones might cost more or less. While high-end devices with cutting-edge technology can cost up to $400, more affordable alternatives start at approximately $100.

You can find comprehensive product information and customer assistance on the official websites of Sony,

Bose, and Apple when looking to buy noise-canceling headphones. Additionally, you may choose from a variety of noise-canceling headphones from different manufacturers at major electronics stores and online marketplaces like Amazon, depending on your tastes and price range.

Portable Bluetooth Speakers

Portable Bluetooth speakers are ideal companions for social events and outdoor lovers. These portable speakers produce rich, clear sound and make listening enjoyable whether you're camping, having a picnic, or hosting a BBQ.

Consider brands that place a high priority on portability, durability, and sound quality when selecting portable Bluetooth speakers. Strong-sounding and toughly built portable speakers from the famous audio company JBL are perfect for outdoor activities. Because they are waterproof and dustproof, Ultimate Ears (UE) speakers are distinguished by their capacity to survive challenging circumstances. An immersive experience is provided by Bose SoundLink Revolve's 360-degree sound dispersion.

Small Bluetooth speakers are priced differently according to factors including sound quality, brand reputation, water resistance, and battery life. Options with fewer features start at roughly $50, while those with more features can cost up to $200.

Visit the official websites of JBL, Ultimate Ears, and Bose for comprehensive product information and customer assistance. Alternatively, you can choose from a large selection of portable Bluetooth speakers to fit your preferences and budget at reputable electronics retailers and online marketplaces like Amazon.

The best way to fully enjoy your favorite music and audio material is to invest in high-quality audio accessories from reliable companies, whether you want noise-canceling headphones for a relaxing listening experience or portable Bluetooth speakers for entertainment on the go.

Chargers and Cables

USB-C Power Adapters

All iPad users need a USB-C power adapter since they offer quick and effective charging capabilities. These power adapters provide a flexible charging solution for the expanding number of USB-C connections in contemporary electronic gadgets, ensuring that your iPad is always charged and available for use.

Think about manufacturers that place an emphasis on numerous USB-C ports and small designs when choosing a USB-C power converter. The adapter's small size makes it portable and perfect for travel, and its several USB-C connections enable you to charge multiple devices at once, saving time and outlet space.

Anker, a reputable brand in the electronics sector, provides a selection of dependable and quick-charging USB-C power adapters. The authentic USB-C Power Adapter from Apple ensures the best compatibility with Apple products and offers reliable charging. Aukey, which is renowned for its cost-effective yet high-quality goods, provides USB-C power adapters at competitive costs without sacrificing performance.

Depending on the manufacturer, wattage, and charging speed, USB-C power adapters can fluctuate in price. While more powerful adapters with cutting-edge capabilities can cost up to $50, basic versions start at approximately $20.

You can find comprehensive product information and customer assistance on the official websites of Anker, Apple, and Aukey for USB-C power adapters. In addition, you may choose from a variety of USB-C power adapters from different manufacturers at major electronics stores and online marketplaces like Amazon, depending on your demands and price range.

Lightning Cables

A dependable Lightning cable that can be used for both charging and data syncing is crucial for a flawless iPad experience. These cables are compatible with numerous Apple products and USB power sources since they have a standard USB connection on one end and an Apple Lightning connector on the other. Choose durable designs with braided cables and stronger connections to prevent fraying and breaking after regular usage. This will assure longevity and top-notch performance. Genuine Apple Lightning-to-USB cables ensure the finest performance and compatibility with Apple products while delivering quick charging and data transfer.

Anker's Lightning Cable is a reliable and reasonably priced alternative to Belkin's Lightning to USB Cable, which is famous for its longevity. Prices range from roughly $10 for simple cables to up to $30 for longer and better designs, depending on length and construction. To satisfy various needs and price ranges, get Lightning cables from official websites or reliable electronics merchants like Amazon. All work and entertainment needs can be met by purchasing durable USB-C power adapters and Lightning connections, among other premium charging accessories.

Other Accessories

Screen Protectors: Screen protectors are essential for all iPad owners because they prevent scuffs and cracks while preserving touchscreen reactivity. Options costing between $10 and $30 are available from companies, including AmFilm, Spigen, and Belkin.

External Drives / SSDs: External drives and SSDs increase iPad storage for content makers, photographers, and videographers who want additional space. Options costing between $100 and $300 are available from brands including Samsung T5 Portable SSD,

Western Digital My Passport SSD, and SanDisk Extreme Portable SSD.

Flash Drives are convenient for on-the-go file transfers and data backup because they are compact and portable storage devices. Options costing $20 to $60 are available from companies including SanDisk iXpand Flash Drive, HooToo iPhone Flash Drive, and Kingston DataTraveler Bolt Duo.

Multiport Adapters: Multiport adapters feature many ports, including HDMI and USB-A, and are ideal for professionals and creatives that want greater connection. Options costing $30 to $100 are available from companies like HyperDrive USB-C Hub, Anker USB-C Hub, and Satechi Multiport Adapter.

SEGUE

With a variety of necessary accessories, this chapter provides insightful advice on how to improve the iPad experience. Protective Cases and Covers from reputable companies like OtterBox, Speck, and Apple Smart Cover / Smart Folio secure the iPad against harm. For professionals and students, keyboard cases turn the device into a laptop-like tool. Sony, Bose, and Apple AirPods Pro noise-canceling headphones are suggested for immersive listening. Outdoor enthusiasts and social groups both greatly benefit from portable Bluetooth speakers. Fast charging is ensured by USB-C Power Adapters, and data syncing and charging are made possible by Lightning Cables. In the following section, "Productivity Tips," we'll look at how to make the most of the iPad's features for effective time management and multitasking on both a personal and business level.

5

PRODUCTIVITY TIPS FOR MANAGING PERSONAL AND PROFESSIONAL TASKS ON THE IPAD

The iPad has always changed the game when it comes to making life easier, blending seamlessly with our everyday routines, and transforming work like never before. The iPad's full potential is unlocked in this chapter, enabling you to work more productively on both personal and business duties. Discover all of the tools and programs it offers to increase productivity. The iPad's sophisticated design conceals strong functionality for both straightforward and difficult tasks, streamlining work and inspiring creativity. This chapter serves as your guide for maximizing the iPad's potential, altering your daily routine, and assisting you in reaching your objectives with unparalleled effectiveness. On your road to productivity, let the iPad be your dependable traveling buddy.

APPS FOR PRODUCTIVITY

Being productive is essential to effectively managing both personal and professional duties in the fast-paced world of today. The iPad is the perfect tool for increasing productivity because of its simple design and robust functionality. This thorough guide covers email, calendar, note-taking, reminders, word processing, mind mapping, habit monitoring, time tracking, and more. It also investigates a variety of productivity software categories and app types available on the iPad.

Email Apps: Gmail and GDrive

- Where to find and access: Gmail and GDrive can be downloaded from the App Store.
- Recommended Apps: Gmail by Google LLC, Google Drive by Google LLC
- Description: Gmail is a popular email service with a straightforward user interface and useful organizational tools. Google Drive allows seamless storage and sharing of files and documents.
- Purpose and Function: Gmail streamlines email management, making it ideal for personal and

professional communication. Google Drive facilitates file storage, collaboration, and easy access across devices.

- Features: Gmail offers a user-friendly inbox with categorized tabs, smart filters, and priority settings. Google Drive provides cloud storage, file organization, real-time collaboration, and document sharing.
- Step-by-step Guide: Utilize the applications by downloading Gmail and GDrive from the App Store and logging in with your Google account.
- Pros and Cons: The pros of Gmail include smart organization, an intuitive interface, and strong spam filtering. The downside is that some advanced features require a paid subscription. Google Drive's pros include ample storage and seamless collaboration, while limitations may be observed when dealing with larger files.
- Price: Both Gmail and Google Drive are free to use, with additional storage options available for purchase.

Calendar App

- Where to find/access: The Calendar app comes built-in with the iPad.

- Recommended App: Apple Calendar (pre-installed).
- Description: Apple Calendar is a default app that provides a visually appealing and easy-to-navigate calendar interface.
- Purpose and Function: Apple Calendar helps users manage events, appointments, and schedules effectively.
- Features: The app integrates with other Apple services, allows multiple calendar creations, supports event invitations, and offers reminders.
- Step-by-step Guide: Access the Calendar app by tapping on the Calendar icon on your iPad's home screen.
- Pros and Cons: Apple Calendar offers seamless integration with other iOS features, but some users may find the customization options limited compared to third-party calendar apps.
- Price: Apple Calendar is pre-installed and available for free.

Notes App: GoodNotes

- Where to find/access: GoodNotes can be downloaded from the App Store.

- Recommended App: GoodNotes by Time Base Technology Limited.
- Description: GoodNotes is a powerful note-taking app designed for digital handwriting and sketching.
- Purpose and Function: Making digital documents, taking handwritten notes, and annotating PDFs are all possible using GoodNotes.
- Features: The app provides a variety of note templates, supports handwriting recognition, and offers smooth note organization.
- Step-by-step Guide: Download GoodNotes from the App Store, launch the app, and start taking notes.
- Pros and Cons: GoodNotes offers advanced note-taking features and seamless syncing across devices. However, the app requires a one-time purchase.
- Price: GoodNotes is a paid app, available at a one-time cost.

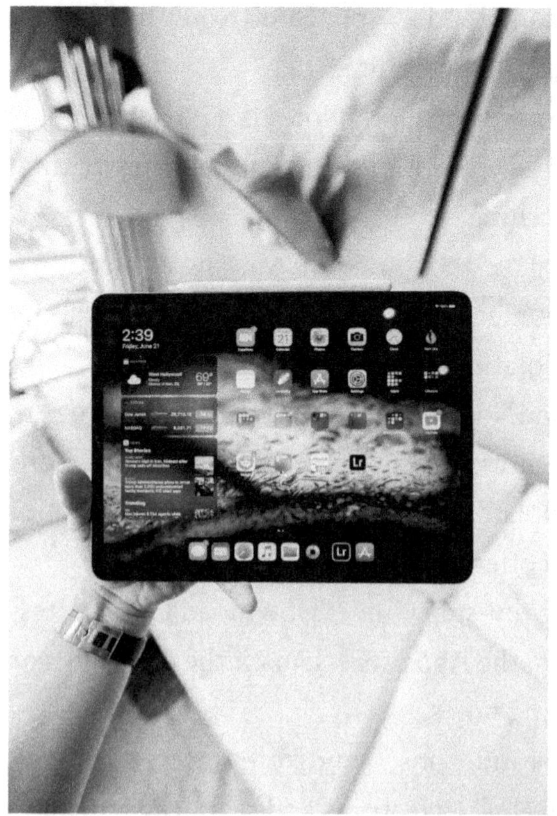

Reminders App

- Where to find/access: The Reminders app comes built-in with the iPad.
- Recommended App: Apple Reminders (pre-installed).
- Description: Apple Reminders is a straightforward app for creating to-do lists and setting reminders.

- Purpose and Function: The app assists in organizing tasks and deadlines efficiently.
- Features: Apple Reminders offers smart lists, subtasks, due dates, and location-based reminders.
- Step-by-step Guide: Access the Reminders app from your iPad's home screen.
- Pros and Cons: Apple Reminders is easy to use, but it may lack advanced features found in some third-party reminder apps.
- Price: Apple Reminders is pre-installed and available for free.

Pages, Numbers, and Keynote Apps

- Where to find/access: Pages, Numbers, and Keynote are pre-installed productivity apps from Apple.
- Recommended Apps: Pages, Numbers, and Keynote (pre-installed).
- Description: Pages is a word processing app, Numbers is a spreadsheet app, and Keynote is a presentation app.
- Purpose/Function: These apps cater to various document creation needs.
- Features: Pages provides templates and advanced formatting options for text documents.

Numbers offers powerful spreadsheet tools, and Keynote supports dynamic presentations.

- Step-by-step Guide: Access Pages, Numbers, and Keynote from your iPad's home screen.
- Pros and Cons: These built-in apps offer compatibility with other Apple devices, but some users might prefer third-party alternatives for specific functionalities.
- Price: Pages, Numbers, and Keynote come pre-installed and are available for free.

File Manager App

- Where to find/access: The Files app comes built-in with the iPad.
- Recommended App: Files (pre-installed).
- Description: The Files app is a central hub for managing files stored on your iPad and cloud storage services.
- Purpose and Function: Files streamline file organization and retrieval.
- Features: The app integrates with iCloud Drive and third-party cloud storage services, allowing easy file transfers and organization.
- Step-by-step Guide: Access the Files app from your iPad's home screen.

- Pros and Cons: The Files app is convenient for basic file management, but some users may prefer third-party file managers with advanced features.
- Price: The Files app is pre-installed and available for free.

Word Processor Apps: Microsoft Word and Google Docs, Sheets, and Slides

- Where to find/access: Microsoft Word and Google Docs, Sheets, and Slides can be downloaded from the App Store.
- Recommended Apps: Microsoft Word by Microsoft Corporation; Google Docs, Google Sheets; and Google Slides by Google LLC.
- Description: Microsoft Word is a popular word processing software, while Google Docs, Sheets, and Slides are part of the Google Workspace suite.
- Purpose/Function: These apps cater to document creation, editing, and collaboration.
- Features: Microsoft Word offers comprehensive text editing features, and Google Docs allows real-time collaborative editing. Google Sheets is for spreadsheet

management, and Google Slides is designed for creating presentations.

- Step-by-step Guide: Download the desired app from the App Store, sign in with your Microsoft or Google account, and begin using the app.
- Pros and Cons: Microsoft Word is feature-rich but may require a subscription for advanced functionalities. Google Docs, Sheets, and Slides excel at collaboration but may lack certain advanced features available in Microsoft Word.
- Price: Microsoft Word requires a Microsoft 365 subscription, while Google Docs, Sheets, and Slides are free to use.

Mind-Mapping Apps

- Where to find or access: Mind mapping apps can be downloaded from the App Store.
- Recommended App: MindNode by IdeasOnCanvas GmbH
- Description: Mind mapping apps allow users to create visual diagrams to represent ideas and concepts.
- Purpose/Function: Mind mapping helps in brainstorming, planning, and organizing thoughts.

- Features: MindNode offers a user-friendly interface, various styles, and easy-to-navigate diagrams.
- Step-by-step Guide: Download MindNode from the App Store, launch the app, and start creating mind maps.
- Pros and Cons: MindNode is versatile and efficient for mind mapping, but some users may prefer other apps depending on specific preferences.
- Price: MindNode offers a free version with in-app purchases for additional features.

Habit Tracker Apps

- Where to find or access: Habit tracker apps can be downloaded from the App Store.
- Recommended App: Streaks by Crunchy Bagel
- Description: Habit tracker apps help users build and track positive habits over time.
- Purpose/Function: Habit trackers support personal development and goal-setting.
- Features: Streaks offer customizable habit tracking, reminders, and motivational features.
- Step-by-step Guide: Download Streaks from the App Store, set up your habits, and begin tracking your progress.

- Pros and Cons: Streaks is user-friendly and visually appealing, but users may explore other habit tracker apps for additional features.
- Price: Streaks is a paid app available at a one-time cost.

Time Tracker Apps

- Where to find or access: Time tracker apps can be downloaded from the App Store.
- Recommended App: Toggl Track by Toggl
- Description: Time tracker apps help monitor and manage time spent on different tasks and projects.
- Purpose and Function: Time trackers boost productivity and assist in time management.
- Features: Toggl Track offers time tracking, reporting, and integration with other productivity tools.
- Step-by-step Guide: Download Toggl Track from the App Store, sign up for an account, and start tracking your time.
- Pros and Cons: Toggl Track is an effective time-tracking solution, but users may explore other apps for more advanced features.
- Price: Toggl Track offers a free version with optional premium plans.

With a number of productivity applications at your disposal, the iPad becomes a potent tool for streamlining personal and business duties. Whether you're handling emails, taking notes, tracking habits, or preparing presentations, the iPad's productivity applications include a wealth of features and functions to help you get the most out of your workflow. You can unleash the entire potential of your iPad and boost your productivity like never before by browsing the recommended applications and knowing their distinct benefits.

PRODUCTIVITY TIPS TO OPTIMIZE WORK AND PERSONAL TASKS

When used properly, the iPad is a flexible gadget that may dramatically increase productivity. The iPad, with its user-friendly design and strong capabilities, provides a plethora of tips and techniques for streamlining both business and personal duties. These productivity suggestions are intended to help you make the most of your iPad's capabilities and enhance your efficiency on a variety of tasks. These simple yet efficient strategies can help you improve your productivity and get the most out of your iPad experience, whether you're handling emails, arranging calendars, taking notes, or working on papers.

Multitasking Using Split View and Slide Over

"Split View" and "Slide Over" are two significant multi-tasking features on the iPad. Split View allows you to run two programs side by side on the screen, making it simple to work on various activities at the same time. Slide Over, on the other hand, enables you to overlay a secondary program on top of the primary one, providing rapid access to commonly used apps without interfering with your productivity. These multitasking capabilities let you transition between programs easily, increasing productivity and ensuring you stay focused and effective at work.

App Switcher

Another useful tool that streamlines app browsing on the iPad is the App Switcher. You may view a visual depiction of recently used applications by double-clicking the Home button or sliding up from the bottom of the screen. This allows you to move quickly between programs, saving time and removing the need to hunt for them on the home screen. The App Switcher is a must-have tool for remaining organized and productive, allowing you to easily begin work where you left off.

Copy and Paste Faster

Using straightforward movements, you can quickly copy and paste text on the iPad. You may copy text by choosing it and pinching it in with three fingers. Just use three fingers to pinch out and paste. These simple movements remove the need for complicated menu navigation, making text editing a joy. This rapid copy-and-paste strategy can help you save time and enhance productivity, whether you're working on papers, emails, or notes.

Personalize Your iPad With Widgets.

Personalizing your iPad with widgets is a terrific way to customize your home screen and quickly access important information. Widgets enable instant access to app features and real-time information on a variety of activities, like calendar events, weather, and to-do lists. Widgets may be added, removed, or rearranged by swiping right on the home screen and selecting "Edit." This customized configuration ensures that the most important information is easily accessible, keeping you informed and organized throughout the day.

Safari Extensions

Safari Extensions improve the capabilities of your iPad's Safari web browser. These add-ons provide extra features and tools to improve online browsing and increase productivity. To activate or disable available extensions, click "Settings," scroll down to "Safari," and then pick "Safari." You may modify your surfing experience and gain access to valuable tools that boost efficiency and productivity by utilizing Safari Extensions.

Live Text

With iOS 15 or later, Live Text adds a significant new feature to the iPad. This feature recognizes and interacts with text in pictures or images using Optical Character Recognition (OCR). You can now copy, paste, translate, and do other things with text in photos, making it easier to extract information and deal with visual material. Simply launch the Photos app, choose an image with text, and then press on the text to interact with it, allowing you to achieve a new level of productivity.

Focus Mode

Focus Mode is a useful customization tool that filters notifications and app alerts depending on the contexts you select. This function helps reduce distractions and allows you to focus on certain activities without interruption. To enable Focus Mode, go to "Settings," then "Focus," and then choose a predefined mode or create your own. You can retain concentration and increase productivity during work or leisure time by setting notifications and app alerts to match your priorities.

SEGUE

Utilizing the iPad's potent capabilities for both work and personal chores is the focus of this chapter. It places emphasis on multitasking, setting customization, and making use of technologies like Split View and Slide Over to increase productivity. Readers gain knowledge about streamlining workflows, interacting with photos via text with Live Text, and maximizing

Safari surfing through extensions. Focus Mode reduces interruptions and helps prioritize tasks. Users can prioritize important work and save time by becoming adept at these tactics. The iPad's entertainment capabilities, such as music, movies, TV shows, games, and ebooks, are the subject of the next chapter. Readers gain knowledge on how to configure and optimize entertainment apps, tailoring their enjoyment to the fullest. With the iPad, readers' leisure time is enhanced as it transitions from a productivity tool to an immersive entertainment hub.

6

USING YOUR IPAD AS YOUR PERSONAL ENTERTAINMENT HUB

Mobile devices have completely changed how people consume material in the digital age. The ultimate all-in-one entertainment hub among them is the iPad. The days of carrying a variety of entertainment gadgets are long gone. The iPad provides unparalleled ease with a huge selection of books, movies, music, and games. The clutter is reduced by seamlessly incorporated entertainment apps, allowing users to customize their experiences and have quick access to their preferred material. This chapter explores the various entertainment choices available on iPads, enabling readers to get the most out of reading, watching, or listening to their chosen media. On this adaptable device, explore the limitless possibilities and build your own individual entertainment library.

APPS FOR ENTERTAINMENT

With a wide variety of apps that appeal to different tastes and interests, the iPad has developed into a powerhouse for entertainment. The iPad's App Store has a vast selection of apps to satiate all entertainment needs, including streaming movies and TV shows as well as music, books, games, and other material. In this thorough review, we'll examine and evaluate the best entertainment applications for iPad users while also outlining their features, benefits, drawbacks, and prices.

Movies, TV shows, and Series

Netflix

The suggested streaming service is Netflix, which can be downloaded from the App Store and offers a huge selection of films, TV episodes, and interesting original material in a variety of genres. Netflix attracts customers with customized profiles, offline downloads, and a strong recommendation engine, with its main focus being binge-watching movies and TV shows. The steps include downloading and activating the app, making an account or logging in, perusing the extensive library, and then just tapping on a preferred title to start viewing. By pressing the Home button, users may leave and keep the app updated from the App Store. The portal offers offline viewing choices and a vast collection, although access does require a membership.

HBO Go

HBO Max is a standout option for people looking for high-end entertainment and is simple to obtain through the App Store. The highly recommended app offers a wide range of HBO original material in addition to a huge number of films and TV episodes from various networks, appealing to a variety of tastes. HBO Max provides offline downloading, parental restrictions, and its own unique HBO Max Originals. It is primarily intended for HBO fans and those seeking exclusive material. Users only need to download the app, sign in with their HBO Max account or TV provider, and then explore and play their preferred content to get going. The app may be easily closed with a single push of the Home button, and regular updates guarantee peak performance. It's important to remember, though, that accessing this platform requires a subscription.

Disney+

Disney, Pixar, Marvel, Star Wars, and National Geographic programming can be found in abundance on the well-known streaming service Disney+. The software is suggested for Disney fans looking for family-friendly entertainment and is accessible for download through the Software Store. Offline downloads, kid-friendly profiles, and Disney+ Originals are some of its highlights. Users must download the app, sign in using their Disney+ accounts, and then browse the enormous selection of titles to access the material. Once chosen, users may enjoy the material of their choice before hitting the Home button to quickly dismiss the app. Despite having unique Disney titles and family-friendly material, the site requires a membership to access them.

Amazon Prime Video

The App Store offers the well-known streaming service Amazon Prime Video for download. Access to a large library of films, TV series, and Amazon Originals is available through the highly recommended app, Amazon Prime Video. It caters primarily to Amazon Prime subscribers and offers a variety of materials to suit different interests. Offline viewing, user profiles, and the useful X-Ray tool are all impressive features. Simply download the app, log in with your Amazon account, explore the extensive library, and play the selected material to get going. Updates are easily accessed via the App Store, and the app may be closed with a single push of the Home button. Although it has a large library, including Amazon Originals, a subscription is required to access all of its features.

Viu

The Software Store is where users can get Viu, a necessary piece of software for fans of Asian dramas and global entertainment. Viu offers a huge selection of well-liked television series and films, with a concentration on Asian dramas and entertainment. Fast streaming keeps users interested, while the offline download and subtitle options offer a smooth watching experience. Explore the extensive content library by downloading the app, creating an account, or logging in. To start viewing, just tap on the title. To end watching, use the Home button. The Software Store makes it simple to update the software. However, access to some material might require a paid subscription.

Hulu

You can get Hulu, a well-regarded streaming service, on the App Store. The suggested app caters to individuals looking for a mix of popular oldies, current TV series, and compelling original material. Delivering current

TV series that are only available on Hulu Originals is its main goal. Multiple user profiles, the ability to download material for offline viewing with a subscription, and optional add-ons for live TV are notable features. Users must download the program, log in with their Hulu account, browse the abundance of episodes and movies, choose a title, and then quickly return to the home screen by clicking the Home button in order to access the enormous library. The most recent TV episodes and its captivating Hulu Originals are two of Hulu's biggest advantages, although it does need a subscription.

Peacock TV

The App Store offers Peacock TV, a flexible streaming service that appeals to both NBC viewers and those looking for free programming. A wide range of entertainment options are available on the app, including movies, TV series, news, sports, and exclusive NBCUniversal content. With a membership, users may access live channels, enjoy offline downloads, and watch a variety of unique series. A step-by-step process is used to guarantee a user-friendly experience: download, sign in or establish an account, browse the library, choose a title to watch, and then quit using the Home button. The free tier has NBC exclusives, which is a pro; the free version has commercials.

Apple TV

With Apple TV pre-installed or easily downloaded from the App Store, iPads can easily access a wide selection of films, TV series, and intriguing Apple Originals. This portal offers premium content and primarily serves customers of the Apple ecosystem. The capability of offline downloading (with a subscription), the practicality of Family Sharing, and unique Apple Originals are some of its noteworthy features. Users may either launch the integrated app or download it, log in with their Apple ID, browse the enormous content catalog, and touch on chosen titles to start viewing. The Home button may be used to exit the program, and the program Store can be used to get updates. The availability of unique content and the seamless connection with Apple devices are undeniably appealing, though a subscription is necessary to access all the features.

VLC Media Player

Through its highly recommended software, VLC for Mobile, VLC Media Player, which is available for download on the Software Store, provides an outstanding range of capabilities. Its adaptability makes it the go-to option for iPad users looking for an all-encompassing media player because it enables smooth playback of multiple music and video formats. Wide format compatibility, easy media sharing through Wi-

Fi, and programmable subtitle choices are notable features. Simple steps to use VLC include downloading the software, importing files over iTunes or Wi-Fi, playing content, and closing the app with the Home button. Despite being acclaimed for being free and open-source and having great format compatibility, it falls short because of the lack of streaming alternatives.

Downloading programs for offline viewing

The option to download material for offline viewing is one of many entertainment applications' main advantages. With this function, users can watch movies and TV episodes without requiring an internet connection, which makes it ideal for trips or locations with spotty service. Follow these general procedures to download material for offline viewing:

1. In the first step, launch your preferred entertainment app (such as Netflix, HBO Max, Disney+, etc.).
2. Locate the film or television program you wish to download.
3. Seek out the download icon or button, which is typically a downward-pointing arrow.
4. Tap the download button to begin downloading the content to your iPad.

5. Once the download is complete, look for the downloaded material in the app's Downloads section.

6. Go to the Downloads area, touch on the title, and start watching to access your downloaded video offline.

Music

iTunes

If you possess an iPad, you'll be happy to learn that iTunes is pre-installed and provides a number of conveniences. iTunes offers a huge variety of songs, movies, and TV shows as Apple's dedicated media player and online shop. It acts as the ideal app for acquiring and maintaining your prized digital media material because it is seamlessly linked into the ecosystem of the iPad. With a simple user interface, iTunes makes it simple to organize your music library, create personalized playlists, and make music purchases. Additionally, the addition of the iCloud Music Library ensures that your material is accessible and enjoyable on your iPad by syncing it across devices.

Step-by-step guide:

1. Open iTunes, explore the iTunes Store, choose the songs you wish to buy, tap the price, and

then follow the on-screen instructions to finish the transaction.

2. To explore your music collection, select the "Library" tab. You may then filter by song, artist, or album and use the search field to locate particular tracks.

3. The "Playlists" tab should be selected before selecting the "+" icon to add a new playlist. After giving your playlist a name, just drag and drop songs from your library into it.

4. To sync your music across all of your Apple devices, turn on iCloud Music Library in Settings > Music.

Pros and Cons:

- Pros: Extensive music library; seamless integration with Apple devices; easy music organization.
- Cons: Purchased music can be costly and is not available on non-Apple devices.

Spotify

Spotify is available on the App Store, making it simple for iOS users to access. Spotify is a well-liked music streaming software that offers a sizable selection of songs and playlists from several artists and genres. Its primary goal is to give customers bespoke playlists based on their tastes and on-demand music streaming. Expertly produced playlists that let users find new tunes and tailored suggestions based on their listening history are some of the app's main features. The premium edition allows offline listening for an uninterrupted music experience, enabling users to listen to their favorite music whenever and wherever they choose.

Step-by-step guide:

1. Search for "Spotify" in the App Store, tap "Get," and install the app.
2. Open the app, sign in or register for a new account, and browse the music collection.
3. To exit the app, press the Home button or swipe up from the bottom.
4. To uninstall an application, tap and hold the icon until it jiggles. Then tap the "x" icon.
5. Go to the App Store, search for "Spotify," and, if it's available, hit "Update."
6. To access Home, Search, Your Library, and Premium features, use the menu at the bottom.
7. Explore playlists and artists, and play, stop, skip, and change the volume of tracks.
8. Create and follow playlists, like songs, share music with friends, and use Spotify's radio feature.

Pros and Cons

- Pros: Extensive music library, personalized playlists, offline listening (premium), cross-platform support.
- Cons: Ads (free version); a premium subscription is required for some features.

Books

Kindle Reading Apps

The Kindle app is highly recommended if you're seeking a handy way to explore the world of books. To get it, visit the App Store. Users of this software, which is powered by Amazon, get quick access to a wide selection of eBooks and audiobooks available on the Kindle Store. It excels at offering an immersive reading experience for voracious readers, with a variety of backdrop colors, font sizes, and the possibility to add bookmarks for simple navigation. Additionally, it provides flawless synchronization between numerous devices, enabling you to continue where you left off regardless of the device you're using. Kindle is the go-to option for the best eBook reading experience and the widest collection of books.

Step-by-step guide:

1. Download: Search for "Kindle" in the App Store, tap "Get," and install the app.
2. Access: Open the app, log in with your Amazon account, and access your Kindle library.
3. Close: Tap the Home button or swipe up from the bottom and swipe the app off the screen.

4. Uninstall: Remove an application by tapping and holding the icon, then tapping the "x" to confirm the deletion.
5. Update: Look up "Kindle" in the App Store and, if it's available, tap "Update."
6. Navigate: Use the menu at the bottom to access the Home, Library, Store, and Search features.
7. Basic Features: Tap on a book cover to start reading; use the navigation bar to flip pages.
8. Unique Features: Highlight text, add notes, and adjust reading settings (font, color, etc.).

Pros and Cons:

- Pros: Extensive eBook collection; customizable reading experience; sync across devices.
- Cons: Not all eBooks are available in Kindle format, which requires an Amazon account.

Streaming Videos or Content

YouTube

YouTube, a widely acclaimed video-sharing platform, can be effortlessly downloaded from the App Store, granting users access to an extensive array of captivating videos. As a top recommendation, YouTube caters to diverse interests, allowing viewers to explore an expansive collection of user-generated content, music videos, and instructive tutorials. Its purpose revolves around enriching users' lives with endless entertainment and educational resources. Through an intuitive interface, YouTube boasts remarkable features, such as personalized video recommendations tailored to individual preferences, the ability to like, comment, and share videos, as well as the convenience of subscribing to favorite content creators. Without a doubt, this feature-rich app is revolutionizing the way we use and engage with digital content.

Step-by-step guide:

- Download: Search for "YouTube" in the App Store, tap "Get," and install the app.
- Access: Open the app, explore trending videos, or search for specific content.
- Close: Tap the Home button or swipe up from the bottom and swipe the app off the screen.
- Uninstall: Tap and hold the app icon, tap the "x" icon, and confirm the deletion.
- Update: Go to the App Store, find "YouTube," and tap "Update" if available.
- Navigate: Use the menu at the bottom to access Home, Trending, Subscriptions, and Library.
- Basic Features: Tap on a video to start watching, use the progress bar to skip, and tap the thumbs-up or down icon to like or dislike.
- Unique Features: Subscribe to channels, create playlists, and discover trending videos.

Pros and Cons:

- Pros: Vast video library; free to use; user-generated content.

- Cons: Ads (free version), limited offline viewing (premium).

TikTok

Install the recommended software from the Software Store in order to utilize TikTok. The popular short-form video app TikTok has engaging material. Users may produce and share creative videos that showcase their ingenuity and ability. TikTok's mission is to provide a platform for short, fascinating videos, to popularize viral trends, and to conduct entertaining challenges. TikTok has an easy-to-use interface and a variety of features, such as video editing tools to enhance videos, a vast music collection to add catchy soundtracks, and the ability to make duets and reactions, promoting interactive and collaborative content production. Accept the fun and excitement of TikTok and become a part of the worldwide community of video creators and viewers.

Step-by-step guide:

1. Download: Search for "TikTok" in the App Store, tap "Get," and install the app.
2. Access: Open the app, sign up for a new account, and explore trending videos.

3. Close: Tap the Home button or swipe up from the bottom and swipe the app off the screen.

4. Uninstall: Tap the app icon while holding down the "x" key to confirm the deletion.

5. Update: Look up "TikTok" in the App Store and, if it's available, tap "Update."

6. Navigate: Use the icons at the bottom to access the Home, Discover, Upload, and Profile tabs.

7. Basic Features: Tap on a video to start watching, swipe up to skip, and tap the heart icon to like videos.

8. Unique Features: Record and edit your videos, use filters, duet with other users, and discover trending challenges.

Pros and Cons:

- Pros: Trending content, creative video-making tools, viral potential.
- Cons: Limited video duration; potential privacy concerns.

Snapchat

You can easily get Snapchat from the App Store by going there. Snapchat is a multimedia messaging service that comes highly recommended and is known for its distinctive features? It provides a riveting experience with its engrossing Stories, entertaining Lenses, and educational Discover section. The main use of the app is to share photographs and videos with friends, which makes it perfect for maintaining relationships and expressing one's creativity. Notable characteristics include messages that vanish after viewing, which adds a sense of thrill and anonymity. Users may also take pleasure in using Bitmojis to create custom avatars that liven up their interactions. In general, Snapchat is the preferred app for social amusement and multimedia communication.

Step-by-step guide:

1. Download: Search for "Snapchat" in the App Store, tap "Get," and install the app.
2. Access: Open the app, sign up or log in with your Snapchat account, and access the camera interface.
3. Close: Tap the Home button or swipe up from the bottom and swipe the app off the screen.
4. Uninstall: To uninstall an app, tap and hold it, tap the "x" icon, and then confirm the deletion.
5. Update: Look up "Snapchat" on the App Store and, if it's available, press "Update."
6. Navigate: Use the icons at the bottom to access the Camera, Chats, Discover, and Snap Map.

7. Basic Features: Tap the circular capture button to take a photo, hold it to record a video, and swipe left or right to apply filters.

8. Unique Features: Create and share Stories with photos and videos; use Lenses and filters; explore and Discover content from publishers.

Pros and Cons:

- Pros: Fun and interactive features; creative photo and video sharing; real-time updates.
- Cons: Content disappears after viewing and may not be suitable for long-form communication.

Games

Variety of Games for All Ages and Genres: The iPad offers a wide variety of games that are appropriate for players of all ages and interests. Its adaptability allows it to be used by children, teenagers, adults, and the elderly, offering a diverse gaming experience. Adventure fans may explore enthralling worlds with games like "The Legend of Zelda: Breath of the Wild," "Minecraft," and "Oceanhorn." Puzzle enthusiasts may exercise their brains with "Monument Valley," "Candy Crush Saga," and "Sudoku." "Solitaire," "Hearthstone," and "Clash Royale" all provide exciting games for card enthusiasts.

Fans of fast reflexes will love "Crossy Road," "Temple Run," and "Jetpack Joyride," while strategy aficionados may lose themselves in "Civilization VI," "Plague Inc.," and "Clash of Clans." Meanwhile, "Final Fantasy XV Pocket Edition," "Bastion," and "Stardew Valley's" fantastical environments entice RPG fans to go out on grand journeys. No matter their age or preferred type of game, everyone can find something to enjoy on the iPad thanks to its enormous game catalog.

Step-by-step guides, features, pros, and cons for individual games will vary, and it's recommended to check the App Store for specific game details.

TIPS TO MAXIMIZE YOUR IPAD AS YOUR FUN BUDDY

The iPad is a strong gadget that might be your ideal entertainment partner. The iPad has a wide range of functions and settings to improve your enjoyment of viewing movies, playing games, listening to music, or reading books. The entertainment possibilities of your iPad will be explored in detail in this book, allowing you to fully appreciate your favorite material.

Multitasking

With the ability to run numerous applications at once on the iPad, multitasking makes it simple to complete different chores while taking in the entertainment.

You could, for instance, view a movie while utilizing other apps, the web, or email while multitasking.

How to Enable or Use It:

1. The App Switcher will appear when you swipe up from the bottom of the screen.
2. Drag the app you want to use for multitasking to the right or left side of the screen.
3. Open the second app from the App Switcher, and it will appear in the split-screen view.
4. Adjust the divider between the two apps to control the screen space for each app.

Automatic Rotate

Depending on how you hold the iPad, the Automatic Rotate function allows your iPad to automatically change the screen orientation.

By using this function, you can be sure that the screen will automatically rotate to the best orientation for your material and deliver a fluid viewing experience.

How to Enable or Use It:

1. Swipe down from the top-right corner of the screen to access the Control Center.
2. Tap the "Lock" icon to enable or disable the Automatic Rotate feature.
3. When the lock icon is highlighted, the screen orientation will not change, and when it's not highlighted, the screen will rotate freely based on device orientation.

Use Your iPad as a Second Monitor With Third-Party Apps

You may utilize your iPad as a second display by extending your computer's desktop to it using third-party apps.

By giving users more screen space for multitasking, showing resources, or working on several projects at once, this feature boosts productivity.

How to Enable or Use It:

1. Download and install a third-party app such as "Duet Display" or "Sidecar."
2. You can connect your iPad to your computer wirelessly (if the program supports it) or with a USB connection.

3. Launch the app on both your iPad and computer, and your iPad will function as a second monitor.

Use the iPad as a Car Entertainment System

Use your iPad as an entertainment center for lengthy vehicle rides by watching movies, playing games, or listening to music.

With the help of this advice, automobile travel may be made more fun and less boring for the passengers.

How to Enable or Use It:

1. Securely mount your iPad to the car's headrest or dashboard using a compatible mount.
2. Download your favorite movies, TV shows, or games to your iPad before the trip (consider

using offline viewing options from streaming apps).

3. Connect your iPad to the car's audio system through Bluetooth or an auxiliary cable for better sound quality.
4. Ensure passengers have headphones for personal audio, if needed.

For Parents: Limiting Video, Movie Streaming, and Games on the iPad

On the iPad, parents may configure limitations and parental controls to prevent access to objectionable content or limit their children's screen time.

With the help of this advice, parents can guarantee that their kids' iPad pleasure is both safe and well-rounded.

How to Enable or Use It:

1. Go to "Settings" on the iPad.
2. Tap on "Screen Time" and set up a passcode if prompted.
3. Tap on "App Limits" to limit the usage of specific app categories like games or entertainment apps.
4. Use "Content & Privacy Restrictions" to control access to age-inappropriate content, restrict explicit language, or disable in-app purchases.

SEGUE

The iPad was transformed into an exciting source of entertainment by the variety of entertainment apps we examined in this chapter. Users could enjoy movies, TV shows, music, and eBooks while on the go, thanks to streaming services like Netflix, HBO Go, and Disney+, as well as music apps like iTunes and Spotify. Short-form videos and user-generated material on social media sites like YouTube, TikTok, and Snapchat increased creativity. Gamers might choose from a variety of games on the App Store. The following chapter investigates communication features, including texting, messaging, video calling, and social media, to broaden users' iPad experiences beyond entertainment and promote deep interactions. The iPad turns into a potent instrument for communication and pleasure, enhancing their online experience.

iPad Practice

"Technology is best when it brings people together."

— MATT MULLENWEG

Let's be honest, an iPad isn't a cheap device... But hopefully, by now, you're beginning to see that you're getting a lot more for your money than you realized.

There are so many possibilities with an iPad, and it's surprising how many users there are out there who don't yet know what theirs can do for them. I want to change that, which is why I wrote this book.

I'd like to invite you to use your iPad now with the express purpose of helping other users – simply by spreading the word.

By leaving a review of this book on Amazon, you'll show other iPad users how much potential their device has, and you'll show them exactly where to find the guidance they need to help them access it.

Here's how.

1. Tap on the link provided
2. Scroll down, and tap 'Customer Reviews'

3. Tap 'Write a Review'
4. Type out your honest feedback on this book in
   the space provided
5. Tap 'Submit'

Simply by letting other readers know how this book has helped you and what they'll find inside, you'll provide a signpost that lets them know where they can find easy-to-read, user-friendly advice that will help them get the most out of their iPad. And, of course, you can also do this on your phone or your laptop – whichever is most convenient for you.

Thank you for your support. It's going to make a huge difference to other iPad users.

Scan the QR code below

7

KEEPING IN TOUCH—TEXTING, MESSAGING, VIDEO CALLING, AND NAVIGATING SOCIAL MEDIA PLATFORMS

Maintaining meaningful relationships with loved ones in today's fast-paced digital world is essential, but keeping up with developing technologies can be difficult. By teaching readers how to use communication features on their iPads efficiently, this chapter strives to close the communication gap. It covers social networking, video calling for immediate contact, messaging apps, emoticons, photographs, and online messaging services for interesting conversations. For those who prefer a more conventional approach, the art of email communication is also examined. Utilizing their iPad to fortify ties and ensure that distance doesn't impede the warmth shared with loved ones, users will confidently navigate the digital world armed with this information.

APPS FOR CONNECTING WITH THE WORLD

In this in-depth overview, we will look at a variety of applications for connecting with the outside world on your iPad. Human connections revolve around communication, and with the aid of social media, texting, and video chatting applications, we can reduce distances, foster relationships, and keep up with the most recent events in our social networks. The iPad offers a wide range of tools to keep us in touch with the outside world, whether it's sharing moments on social media, having in-the-moment talks through texting, or enjoying face-to-face encounters via video calls.

Apps for Social Media

Facebook

Facebook continues to be one of the most popular social networking sites, and it is available via the iPad's App Store or Safari browser. It lets users connect with friends and family, take part in a variety of groups, and follow interesting pages while sharing updates, images, and videos with ease. The News Feed, Timeline, Groups, Pages, and Messenger are just a few of the numerous services that Facebook offers, with a major focus on establishing community and keeping connected. A vital tool for social interaction in the digital age, its user-friendly layout makes it the go-to app for sharing life's experiences, sustaining connections, and connecting with a larger online community.

Twitter

The top microblogging platform is Twitter, which can be downloaded from the App Store. Users like the suggested app for its ease of use and effectiveness in posting succinct updates, known as tweets, and keeping connected to hot subjects, breaking news, and powerful people. Twitter, which focuses mostly on giving real-time information, comes in handy for following the most recent events and taking part in heated debates. Retweeting, using hashtags to group material, mentioning other users, creating lists for structured following, and having private chats via direct messaging are just a few of the capabilities available on the site. Twitter continues to be an unrivaled tool for expressing views and keeping up with current events in a world that values conciseness and fast communication.

Instagram

The most popular photo and video-sharing app is Instagram, which can be downloaded from the App Store. On this platform, visual material, and narrative take center stage. The seamless sharing of photographs, quick films, and gripping tales is key to its mission of building relationships via artistic expression. Instagram provides users with the ideal experience because of its extensive feature set. People may find and interact with content from friends and accounts they've followed on The Feed. Stories give fleeting insights into users' lives, but IGTV is geared for long-form videos. Reels provide a venue for entertaining and inventive short videos. Additionally, Direct Messages allow for private interactions, and Explore offers a wealth of fascinating and motivating discoveries.

Clubhouse

Clubhouse is a novel audio-based social networking platform that transforms how individuals participate in live discussions. It is presently accessible through the App Store and compatible with the iPhone and iPad. Users may explore a variety of topics by hosting or attending audio rooms on the highly rated Clubhouse app, which fosters a climate that is favorable to deep talks. The platform offers a great way to interact with others who share your interests and fosters relationships and teamwork within a worldwide community. Users can easily curate their interests, take part in thought-provoking debates, and widen their social networks with the help of essential features like Audio Rooms, Clubs, Follows, and Invites, which make Clubhouse a unique and dynamic location in the world of social media.

Reddit

The top forum-based platform, known as the "front page of the internet," is Reddit, which is accessible on the App Store as the top-rated app. It serves as a comprehensive center for a variety of issues by allowing users to participate in a variety of debates. The platform's goals include encouraging participation in specialized groups, acting as a clearinghouse for assistance requests, and allowing users to browse a wide variety of material. Subreddits, one of the site's key features, classify topics, while Posts and Comments encourage lively debate. Additionally, the voting mechanism gives users discretion over what material is seen. Reddit is an essential site for information exchange, discovery, and networking with like-minded people because of its adaptability and user-driven structure.

Pinterest

A famous visual discovery site called Pinterest, which can be downloaded from the App Store, is a refuge for gathering and archiving a ton of creative ideas. With its easy-to-use interface, Pinterest enables users to browse and bookmark information on a variety of subjects, from imaginative designs and delectable recipes to fascinating DIY projects. The main functions of the program, such as Pins, Boards, Explore, and Save, let users create custom collections of pictures and articles, creating an online environment that represents their interests and goals. Pinterest is a flexible platform that makes it easy to organize creativity, making it a priceless source for anybody looking for ideas and useful advice.

LinkedIn

LinkedIn, which can be downloaded from the App Store, is the preferred professional networking site for people looking to create and develop meaningful relationships while looking for new employment. LinkedIn offers users a thorough experience with its user-friendly interface, offering crucial features like customized profiles, the ability to connect with peers and professionals in the field, participating in insightful discussions through posts, and practical messaging options to stay in touch with contacts. Additionally, its job search function helps job seekers find pertinent employment prospects and keep up with market developments. LinkedIn continues to be a crucial resource for both aspiring professionals and seasoned professionals alike, emphasizing the importance of professional networking, job searching, and industry insights.

Messaging and Video Calling Apps

FaceTime

Apple's leading video and audio calling service, Face-Time, is built-in software for the iPad that enables seamless communication across Apple devices. Highly recommended for its user-friendliness and high-quality audio and video for seamless interactions. Its main objective is to establish video and audio connections among iOS users in order to customize online chats. Users may easily keep in touch with one another via FaceTime, whether it be one-on-one or in a group situation. The software also includes quirky components like Animoji and Memoji, bringing a humorous twist to chats. With FaceTime's variety of capabilities, including video calls, voice calls, group FaceTime, and Animoji and Memoji, communicating with family and friends is made more enjoyable.

Telegram

Telegram is a highly recommended piece of software that is readily available through the Software Store. It is a secure messaging network with a focus on privacy and quick message delivery. This adaptable program excels at private chats, enabling secure messaging with its exclusive "Secret Chats" function. Additionally, Telegram encourages fluid communication among diverse social groups by allowing users to participate in lively group chats via "Channels" and "Groups." For a complete communication experience, the app's functionality also includes practical voice calls and effective file sharing. Because of its dedication to privacy and extensive feature set, Telegram is a popular option for both individuals and organizations looking for a dependable messaging service.

WhatsApp

The messaging program WhatsApp, which is free to download from the program Store, is highly recommended. Due to its adaptability in supporting text, audio, and video conversations, all of which are strengthened by end-to-end encryption for increased security, it has great appeal. The main goal of the software is to make personal and group chat easier while promoting fluid user interaction. Additionally, it provides a dependable platform for audio and video communications, enabling customers to keep in touch with friends and family wherever they are in the world. WhatsApp is a must-have tool for contemporary communication requirements because of its extensive feature set, which also includes Chats for private and group talks, Calls for audio and video interactions, Status for posting updates, and practical File posting options.

Messenger

As Facebook's main messaging service, Messenger, which can be downloaded from the App Store, lets users communicate with Facebook friends via text, audio, and video conversations. The suggested program, Facebook Messenger, offers a variety of features for interesting conversations, making it the perfect tool for smooth communication. Users have the option of having real-time chats using Chats, making voice calls, or choosing video calls for face-to-face encounters. With the help of Reactions and Stickers, Messenger's fun and expressive features, people can easily express their feelings. Additionally, users may amuse themselves with in-app Games, which spice up their texting experience with a little fun. Within the Facebook ecosystem, Messenger thrives as a complete communication center because of its user-friendly design and plenty of functions.

Mail

Apple's primary email client, "Mail," which is handy built-in software on the iPad, is available for use. Mail makes email communication simpler by enabling simple sending, receiving, and management of emails thanks to its user-friendly design. It is advised to remain with the Mail app that comes with your device for a smooth experience. Its main objective is to easily manage numerous email accounts and streamline email-related duties. Users may take advantage of a number of useful functions, including creating new messages, searching for certain emails, and creating folders to organize their correspondence. Mail demonstrates itself to be a flexible and essential tool for staying connected and on top of your email game, whether for personal or business use.

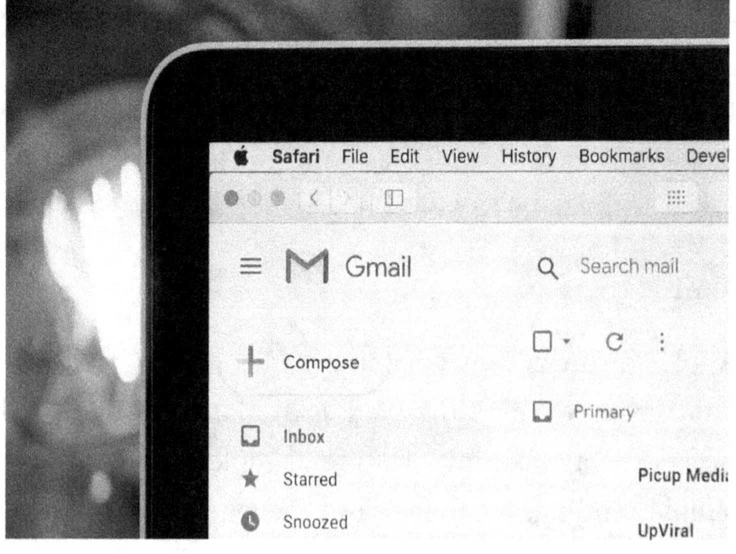

Gmail

Users of iPad devices may easily access their Gmail accounts using Gmail, the well-known email service from Google. The suggested program, Gmail, is easily downloaded from the program Store and provides a user-friendly interface for quickly handling emails. It offers easy control of all email-related operations, including sending, receiving, and organizing messages. It was created with the intention of catering to Gmail users. Gmail provides an efficient and organized email management experience for iPad users with a wide range of tools at its disposal, including the capacity to send and receive emails, apply labels, implement filters, and execute rapid searches.

Google Meet

Google Meet is a highly-rated video conferencing software that can be accessed through the App Store and is appropriate for both professional and social gatherings. It enables flawless virtual meetings, webinars, and events because of its user-friendly design. With crucial capabilities like video calls, Google Meet enables users to meet face-to-face regardless of where they are. Screen-sharing options support presentations and group discussions, while the recording capability allows users to capture significant sessions for future reference. Additionally, the platform's Breakout Rooms feature enables more concentrated interactions by allowing for smaller group conversations inside larger meetings. As a flexible and dependable solution for contemporary communication demands, Google Meet stands out.

Skype

The app Store makes Skype a simple download, making it a standout as a suggested program for smooth communication. Skype connects users with their Skype connections as well as landlines thanks to its many capabilities, which enable both video and voice calling. Its main goals are to eliminate barriers to international calling, simplify video conferencing, and promote real-time texting. With its extensive feature set, Skype enables users to communicate via phone, video, and text, in addition to offering the ease of screen-sharing. Skype serves as a vital tool for maintaining contact with friends, family, and coworkers throughout the world since it is a dependable and user-friendly platform.

Zoom

Zoom is a popular video conferencing program that can be downloaded from the program Store and is the preferred choice for online meetings, webinars, and teamwork. Zoom has established itself as a key tool for organizing video meetings, virtual events, and distant collaborations because of its user-friendly design and smooth connectivity. Participants may engage in fruitful conversations and cooperation from any place thanks to the app's outstanding array of features, which include video calls, screen-sharing, recording capabilities, and practical breakout rooms. When it comes to collaborating with coworkers around the world or running interactive webinars, Zoom has cemented its reputation as a flexible and essential tool in the contemporary digital landscape.

Discord

Discord, which can be downloaded from the program Store, stands out as the voice and chat program that is suggested for both social groups and gamers. Its main objective is to promote natural communication among gamers via text, audio, and video channels. Discord, a messaging app targeted at gamers, offers a variety of tools to improve collaboration, including servers that act as virtual meeting spaces, channels for grouping talks, voice calls for in-context chats, and screen-sharing for teamwork. This multidimensional platform has cemented its status as a vital resource for contemporary gaming communities and beyond, becoming the go-to option for individuals looking for a user-friendly and feature-rich communication center.

Built-in Messaging and Call Apps (For iPad Models With Data or Mobile Cellular Connectivity)

Messages

- Access: Built-in app on iPad
- Description: Messages is Apple's built-in messaging app for sending text messages and iMessages to other Apple users.
- Purpose: Best for text messaging with other iOS users, including group chats.
- Features: Text Messages, iMessages, Photos, and animoji and memoji.

Calls

- Access: Built-in app on iPad with data or mobile cellular connectivity
- Description: The Calls app on the iPad allows users to make and receive voice calls using the device's cellular capabilities.
- Purpose: Ideal for making and receiving traditional voice calls to non-iOS users or landlines.
- Features: Phone Calls, Contacts, Call History, Voicemail, and Call Waiting

Step-by-Step Guide for Built-in Messaging and Call Apps

Sending and Replying to Messages

- Launch the messaging app.
- By tapping the "Compose" button and entering the recipient's name or phone number, a new message can be sent.
- Once you've finished typing, press the "Send" button.
- You can respond to a message by tapping on the conversation, typing your comment in the text field, and then selecting "Send."

Placing a Call

- Get the Calls app open.
- Using the keypad, dial the number you wish to call.
- To make the call, tap the green "Call" button.

Answering a Phone Call

- When receiving a phone call, swipe the green phone icon to answer.
- Alternatively, tap "Accept" when the call screen appears.

Setting up a voicemail message

- Call your voicemail by pressing and holding the "1" key on the keypad.
- Follow the prompts to set up your voicemail message.

Deleting Messages

- Open the Messages app.
- Swipe left on the message you want to delete and tap "Delete."

Blocking Unwanted Phone Numbers

- Go to "Settings" > "Phone" or "Messages" > "Blocked Contacts."
- Tap "Add New" and enter the phone number or contact you want to block.

Answering the Second Incoming Call

- When on a call, a second incoming call will be displayed as a notification.
- You can choose to "Hold and Accept" the new call or "Decline" it.

Placing a call on Hold

- To put a call on hold while on one, touch the "Hold" button.
- Press the "Hold" button once more to pick up the call.

Pros and Cons

Social Media Apps

- Pros: Stay connected with friends and family, explore diverse content, discover new interests, and build professional connections.

- Cons: Potential privacy concerns, excessive screen time, and exposure to misinformation.

Messaging and Video Calling Apps

- Pros: Seamless communication, real-time interaction, group chats for collaboration, and cost-effective international calls.
- Cons: Reliance on internet connectivity, limited accessibility for non-smartphone users, and potential security risks

Built-in Messaging and Call Apps:

- Pros: Convenience of built-in apps, compatibility with iOS devices, and straightforward user interface.
- Cons: Limited features compared to third-party apps, restricted to the iOS ecosystem, and limited international calling options.

Price

- Social media apps are generally free to download and use.

- Messaging and video calling apps may offer free basic features, but some advanced features may require in-app purchases or subscriptions.
- Built-in messaging and call apps are included with the iPad and do not require additional costs.

TIPS TO CONNECT WITH ANYONE, ANYWHERE, ANYTIME

Thanks to the power of technology, communication with family, friends, and the rest of the globe is simpler than ever in today's linked society. The iPad is a crucial tool for staying in touch with anybody, anywhere, and at any time, thanks to its extensive selection of communication tools and functions. This extensive tutorial will go through many suggestions to make the most of your iPad's potential for fluid communication. These pointers can improve your connectivity experience and help you stay connected with confidence, from making the most of Siri's call and messaging capabilities to protecting yourself from fraud and fraudulent communications.

Limiting Social Media Usage for Parents

To ensure that their children receive a balanced amount of screen time, parents might impose limits on their use of social media.

The iPad's Screen Time feature enables parents to control app usage and place restrictions on social networking sites in order to minimize children's exposure to screen time.

Parents may promote a healthy digital lifestyle for their kids by setting social media usage limits for them and ensuring they have time for other hobbies and face-to-face contacts.

How to Enable or Use It:

- Go to "Settings" > "Screen Time" on the iPad.
- Tap on "App Limits" and set a time limit for social media apps.
- Adjust the duration and customize the schedule based on your preferences.

Using Siri to Optimize Receiving and Making Calls and Messages

Make use of Siri's voice commands to enable hands-free messaging and calling.

Apple's speech assistant, Siri, can carry out a variety of activities and orders using only your voice as input.

You don't need to physically type or use the iPad's UI to make calls, send messages, or dictate texts when you use Siri.

How to Enable or Use It:

- If your iPad supports it, launch Siri by saying "Hey Siri" or by holding down the home button.
- To make a call, say, "Hey Siri, call [contact name]."
- To send a message, say, "Hey Siri, send a message to [contact name] saying [message]."

Recognizing and Avoiding Phishing Messages, Phony Support Calls, and Other Scams

In order to safeguard your personal information and funds, be on the lookout for scams and educate yourself about them.

Scammers frequently employ a variety of strategies, including phishing emails and false support calls, to deceive people into disclosing personal information or making fraudulent purchases.

You can protect yourself and your loved ones from falling victim to internet fraud by being aware of these scams and being able to spot them.

How to Enable or Use It:

- Be wary of calls or messages asking for personal or financial information.
- By immediately dialing the relevant company's official customer service number, you can confirm the legitimacy of support calls.
- Use secure payment options and refrain from clicking on shady links in emails or communications.

SEGUE

In this chapter, we looked at iPad apps for communicating with others, including message and video calling services and social media websites. Users of well-known social networking platforms may interact with friends and discover a variety of material using applications like Facebook, Twitter, Instagram, Clubhouse, Reddit, Pinterest, and LinkedIn. FaceTime, Telegram, WhatsApp, Messenger, Mail, Gmail, Google Meet, Skype, Zoom, and Discord are a few examples of messaging and video calling applications that provide easy connection with friends, family, and coworkers.

Reliable phone calls and text messaging are provided via built-in messaging and call programs like Messages and Calls. The following chapter, "Educational Apps and Resources," explores how the iPad may help you learn and develop your skills in a variety of areas.

8

KNOWLEDGE AT YOUR FINGERTIPS—EDUCATIONAL APPS AND RESOURCES

Bring your iPad's full potential as a cutting-edge learning environment and limitless library to life. With the help of this chapter, set out on a voyage of discovery as you explore educational materials and mobile apps that will help you develop your skills and thinking. Explore the limitless opportunities tailored to your academic and professional advancement, from language learning to interactive simulations and study tools. Take charge of your educational path, make the most of the iPad's groundbreaking possibilities, and develop your knowledge and talents to new levels. Prepare yourself for a learning adventure that will alter your life with the knowledge at your fingertips.

APPS FOR KNOWLEDGE AND SKILL BUILDING

Learning has never been more convenient and interesting, thanks to the wide variety of educational applications at your disposal. These applications are made for learners of various ages and interests, from young toddlers to college students and beyond. The iPad also provides a wide range of ebook alternatives, online classes, tutorials, brain-training apps, educational games, and drawing programs, all of which contribute to a thorough learning experience.

Educational Apps

For children, Duolingo is an excellent app. An online program called Duolingo provides classes in many different languages and does it in a gamified way. With regard to language learning or skill improvement for kids, Duolingo is the best option.

Features: To encourage young learners, the app has short lessons, speaking activities, and incentives.

For Teenagers or High School students, Google Classroom is a suggested app that helps teachers create and manage lessons, have conversations, and give comments to students online. High school students who wish to stay organized and efficiently engage with their professors and peers should use this program.

Features: Within the app, students may access course materials, turn in homework, and get teacher comments.

For College or University Students

PhotoMath Definition: PhotoMath is a helpful app that scans arithmetic problems using the device's camera and offers detailed solutions. The goal of PhotoMath is to help college and university students grasp difficult issues and verify their arithmetic homework.

Features: The software covers a wide range of mathematical topics and offers thorough justifications for each step of the solution.

Another recommended App: TutorEva, a personalized tutoring software that links students with knowledgeable instructors for one-on-one learning sessions. It is highly recommended. Use TutorEva to receive individualized help and direction in a range of areas for college and university students.

Features: include the ability to plan sessions, monitor progress, and get personalized study materials.

These educational apps can be downloaded from the App Store.

Step-by-Step Guide:

1. On your iPad, click the App Store icon.
2. Look up the app using its name.
3. Click the app to see more information.
4. To download the app, click "Get" or the app's pricing.
5. Use Touch ID or Face ID for authentication, or enter your Apple ID password.
6. Wait as the iPad downloads and installs the software

How to Open or Access Apps: After downloading an app, tap its icon on the iPad's home screen to open it.

How to Close Apps: Swipe up from the bottom of the screen and hold your finger there to end an app. To close an app, swipe it up and off the screen after finding it by swiping left or right.

How to Uninstall Apps: Press and hold the app icon on the home screen until all the icons start jiggling. To uninstall an app, tap the "X" in the top-left corner and then confirm your choice.

How to Update Apps: Apps can be updated automatically if you have enabled this feature in your iPad's settings. The App Store should be opened, your profile picture should be in the upper right, and you should scroll down to check for any updates that are available. To update an app, click "Update" next to it.

Navigating the App: The layout of each app may vary, but most educational apps have a user-friendly interface with easy-to-access menus and buttons. Look for icons or labels representing different sections or functions of the app.

Pros and Cons: The pros of educational apps include their interactive nature, flexibility, and ability to cater to individual learning styles. They can make learning more enjoyable and convenient. However, some apps may lack comprehensive content or require a stable internet connection.

Price: Duolingo and Google Classroom are free to use. PhotoMath and TutorEva may offer free versions with limited features, but full functionality may require a subscription or in-app purchases.

Ebooks

Recommended Apps: Apple Books, Amazon Kindle, Bluefire, and Google Play Books. Access to a huge collection of digital books, magazines, and other reading materials is made possible via ebook apps. The ability to read books on an iPad, thanks to ebook apps, provides ease and portability for voracious readers. You can get these ebook apps from the App Store.

Step-by-Step Guide (for non-built-in apps):

1. On your iPad, click the App Store icon.
2. Look up the ebook app using its name.
3. Click the app to see more information.
4. To download the app, click "Get" or the app's pricing.
5. Use Touch ID or Face ID for authentication, or enter your Apple ID password.
6. Wait as the iPad downloads and installs the software.

How to Open or Access Apps: Apps can be accessed or opened by tapping their icons on the iPad's home screen after downloading them.

How to Close Apps: Swipe up from the bottom of the screen and pause in the middle to close an app. Find the app you want to exit by swiping left or right, then swipe it up and off the screen.

How to Uninstall Apps: When all the icons on the home screen begin to jiggle, press and hold the app icon. To uninstall an app, tap the "X" in the top-left corner and then click "Install."

How to Update Apps: If you have this feature turned on in your iPad's settings, apps can be updated automatically. Open the App Store, select your profile image in the top right, and scroll down to check available updates to manually update an app. The app you wish to update has "Update" next to it.

Navigating the App: Each ebook app features an easy-to-use user interface that enables users to browse and buy books, organize their collections, and change reading preferences (such as font size and brightness).

Pros and Cons: Ebook apps provide instant access to a vast selection of reading materials, saving space and reducing the need for physical books. However, some readers may miss the tactile experience of holding a physical book.

Price: Ebook apps are generally free to download, and users can purchase ebooks within the app at varying prices, depending on the title and edition. Some ebooks may be available for free.

Online Courses

Recommended Apps: Coursera, LinkedIn Learning, Khan Academy, Udemy, and Skillshare Online course applications provide a wide variety of courses on various topics taught by professionals and experts. Those looking to learn new skills, grow in their jobs, or research certain topics of interest should use these applications. These online course apps can be downloaded from the App Store.

Step-by-Step Guide (for non-built-in apps):

1. On your iPad, click the App Store icon.
2. Use the name of the online course app to find it.
3. Click the app to see more information.
4. To download the app, click "Get" or the app's pricing.
5. Use Touch ID or Face ID for authentication, or enter your Apple ID password.
6. Wait as the iPad downloads and installs the software.

How to Open or Access Apps: After downloading an app, tap its icon on the iPad's home screen to launch it.

Close Apps: Swipe up from the bottom of the screen and pause in the middle to close an app. Swipe left or right to identify the app you want to close, then swipe up to remove it from the screen.

Uninstalling Apps: Hold down the app icon on the home screen until all of the icons begin to jiggle. Tap the "X" in the top-left corner of the app you wish to remove, then confirm the action.

How to Update Apps: If you allow this function in your iPad's settings, apps will be automatically updated. To manually update an app, launch the App Store, navigate to your profile image in the upper right corner, and scroll down to check for available updates. Tap "Update" next to the app that needs to be updated.

Navigating the App: To enroll in courses, access course materials, and track progress, online course applications often provide course categories, search functionality, and a user-friendly interface.

Pros and Cons: Online course apps provide users with flexible learning options, allowing them to study at their own speed and select from a wide selection of subjects. Some courses, however, may not provide the same amount of interaction as traditional classroom environments.

Price: These online course apps may be free to download, but course prices vary. Some courses offer free content, while others require payment for full access.

Tutorials

Recommended App: YouTube Tutorials Definition: YouTube is a video-sharing platform with a vast repository of tutorials on diverse topics. Purpose: YouTube tutorials cater to learners seeking visual demonstrations and step-by-step instructions for various tasks and skills. YouTube may be accessed using the iPad's web browser or downloaded from the App Store.

Step-by-Step Guide (for non-built-in apps):

1. On your iPad, go to the App Store.
2. Look up the YouTube app by name.
3. More information is available by tapping on the app.

4. To download the app, tap "Get" or the app's pricing.
5. For authentication, enter your Apple ID password or use Touch ID or Face ID.
6. Allow enough time for the app to download and install on your iPad.

How to Open or Access Apps: After downloading an app, tap its icon on the iPad's home screen to open it.

How to Close Apps: To close an app, swipe up from the bottom of the screen and pause in the middle. Swipe left or right to find the app you want to close, and then swipe it up and off the screen.

How to Uninstall Apps: Press and hold the app icon on the home screen until all the icons start jiggling. Tap the "X" on the top-left corner of the app you want to uninstall, and then confirm the action.

How to Update Apps: Apps can be updated automatically if you have enabled this feature in your iPad's settings. To manually update an app, open the App Store, go to your profile picture on the top right, and scroll down to see available updates. Tap "Update" next to the app you want to update.

Navigating the App: The YouTube app has a search bar to find specific tutorials, and users can subscribe to channels to access content from their favorite creators.

Pros and Cons: YouTube tutorials offer a vast range of instructional videos on nearly every topic imaginable. However, the platform may also contain misleading or inaccurate content, so users should be discerning in their choices.

Mind-Building Apps

Recommended App: Elevate Definition: Elevate is a brain training app designed to enhance cognitive skills such as memory, focus, and problem-solving. Purpose: Elevate is ideal for individuals seeking to challenge and improve their mental abilities through short, daily exercises. From the App Store, you can get the Elevate app.

Step-by-Step Guide:

1. On your iPad, click the App Store icon.
2. Use the name of the Elevate app to find it.
3. Click the app to see more information.
4. To download the app, click "Get" or the app's pricing.
5. Use Touch ID or Face ID for authentication, or enter your Apple ID password.
6. Wait as the iPad downloads and installs the software.

How to access or Access Apps: After downloading an app, tap its icon on the iPad's home screen to access it.

Close Apps: Swipe up from the bottom of the screen and pause in the middle to close an app. Swipe left or right to identify the app you want to close, then swipe up to remove it from the screen.

Uninstalling Apps: Hold down the app icon on the home screen until all of the icons begin to jiggle. Tap the "X" in the top-left corner of the app you wish to remove, then confirm the action.

How to Update Apps: If you enable this function in your iPad's settings, apps will be automatically updated. To manually update an app, launch the App Store, navigate to your profile image in the upper right corner, and scroll down to check for available updates. Tap the "Update" button next to the app you wish to update.

Navigating the App: Elevate provides a personalized training program with various challenges that adapt to the user's performance and progress.

Pros and Cons: Elevate can be an enjoyable way to boost cognitive skills, but users should supplement it with other mental activities for a well-rounded mind-building experience.

Educational Games

Educational games can be found on the App Store and downloaded like any other app. They offer a fun and interactive way to learn new concepts, enhance problem-solving skills, and reinforce knowledge.

Drawing Apps

Recommended App: Procreate Definition: Procreate is a professional-grade drawing app that provides a wide range of tools and features for digital artists. Purpose: Procreate is ideal for artists, designers, and hobbyists looking to create stunning digital artwork on their iPad. You can get the Procreate app from the App Store.

Step-by-Step Guide:

1. On your iPad, click the App Store icon.
2. By using its name, look for the Procreate software.
3. Click the app to see more information.
4. To download the app, click "Get" or the app's pricing.
5. Use Touch ID or Face ID for authentication, or enter your Apple ID password.
6. Wait as the iPad downloads and installs the software.

How to access or Access Apps: After downloading an app, tap its icon on the iPad's home screen to access it.

Close Apps: Swipe up from the bottom of the screen and pause in the middle to close an app. Swipe left or right to identify the app you want to close, then swipe up to remove it from the screen.

Uninstalling Apps: Hold down the app icon on the home screen until all of the icons begin to jiggle. Tap the "X" in the top-left corner of the app you wish to remove, then confirm the action.

How to Update Apps: If you have this option turned on in your iPad's settings, apps can update automatically. The App Store should be opened, and your profile picture should be in the upper right. You should scroll down to check for any updates that are available. By selecting "Update" next to the app you wish to update.

Navigating the App: Procreate offers an intuitive user interface with customizable brushes, layers, and other advanced tools for creating digital art.

Pros and Cons: Procreate provides powerful tools and features for professional artists and enthusiasts. However, its extensive capabilities may be over-whelming for beginners.

Price: Procreate is a paid app available for purchase from the App Store.

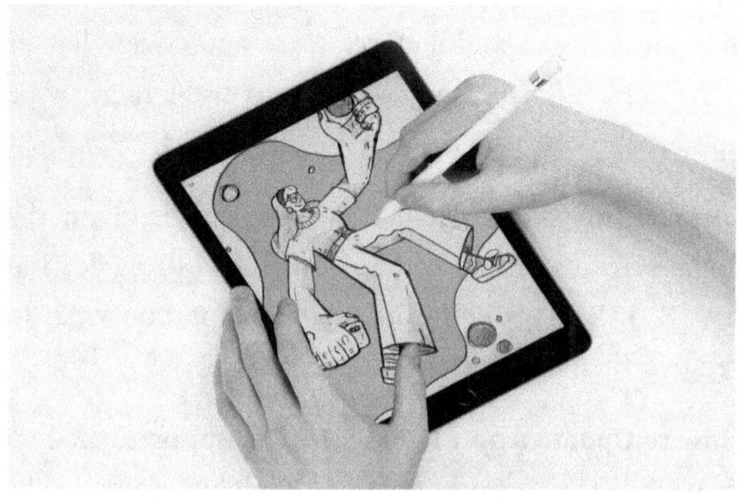

MAXIMIZING THE IPAD AS THE ULTIMATE EDUCATIONAL RESOURCE

The iPad has transformed how we access and acquire knowledge, making it a flexible and effective tool for education. The iPad has a plethora of specialized uses that cater to varied learning requirements, from students to parents, therapists, and elderly folks. This extensive guide will examine how the iPad may be used as a one-stop resource for acquiring new information and skills.

Using the iPad for School and Learning

Studying

Students' access to a wide range of educational tools and materials via the iPad can greatly improve their learning experience.

The iPad comes with a number of settings, applications, and built-in capabilities that make learning more efficient.

Students may use the iPad to browse digital textbooks, take notes, make flashcards, set reminders, and consolidate their study materials.

How to Enable or Use It:

1. Download ebooks or access digital versions of textbooks through apps like Apple Books or Amazon Kindle. Mark important topics using the options for underlining and taking notes.
2. Use the iPad's built-in Notes app or other note-taking apps like Notability or Evernote to jot down lecture notes, ideas, and insights.
3. Create digital flashcards using apps like Quizlet or Anki. These apps allow you to review key concepts, terms, and definitions conveniently.

4. Use the built-in Reminders and Calendar apps
   to set study schedules, assignment deadlines,
   and exam dates.

Writing, Reading, and Reviewing Essays

The iPad is a useful tool for writing, reading, and critiquing essays because of its mobility and multitasking features.

The iPad has a selection of reading and writing apps that facilitate the creation, editing, and annotation of documents.

Essay writing, finding resources for research, and reviewing drafts are all simple tasks for students.

How to Enable or Use It:

1. Writing: Use the iPad's built-in Pages app or
   other writing apps like Microsoft Word or
   Google Docs to create and edit essays. The
   virtual keyboard or an external keyboard can be
   used for typing.
2. Reading: Download research papers, articles,
   and ebooks for reading on the iPad. Apps like
   Apple Books, Kindle, or PDF readers provide a
   comfortable reading experience.

3. Reviewing: Annotate and highlight text within documents using the Markup feature on the iPad or dedicated PDF annotation apps like Adobe Acrobat Reader.

For Parents and Therapists: Using iPads for Children With Communication Difficulties

Children who struggle to communicate, such as those with autism spectrum disorders or speech and language impairments, can utilize the iPad as an aid to communication.

It helps people communicate with others, improves language abilities, and allows youngsters who are nonverbal or barely vocal to express themselves.

How to Enable or Use It:

1. AAC Apps (Augmentative and Alternative Communication): Download specialized AAC apps like Proloquo2Go or TouchChat, which offer customizable communication boards, symbol-based vocabularies, and voice output to assist children in expressing their needs and thoughts.
2. Visual Schedules: Use the iPad to create visual schedules and routines using apps like Choiceworks or First-Then Visual Schedule.

These tools can help children understand and follow daily activities and tasks.

3. Language Learning Apps: Install language learning apps like Speech Blubs or Toca Boca for interactive and engaging language development activities.

Improving Thinking Ability in Older and Senior Adults

The iPad may be used by elderly people as a tool for cognitive training that improves mental acuity and brain health.

Memory, focus, and critical thinking abilities can be enhanced through cognitive training activities and software.

How to Enable or Use It:

1. Brain-Training Apps: Download brain-training apps like Lumosity or Elevate that offer a range of exercises designed to challenge different cognitive abilities.
2. Puzzle Games: Install puzzle games like Sudoku, crossword puzzles, or word search apps to stimulate problem-solving skills.
3. Memory Apps: Utilize memory games and apps like Peak or CogniFit Memory to enhance memory retention and recall.

The iPad as the Ultimate Educational Resource

The iPad's multifunctional capabilities and user-friendly interface make it an invaluable educational resource for learners of all ages. Whether a student, parent, or senior adult, the iPad can be tailored to meet diverse learning needs. As we harness technology for education, the iPad offers a world of knowledge and skills at our fingertips. Embracing its special uses and exploring educational apps maximizes its potential as the ultimate tool for continuous learning and personal growth.

SEGUE

The chapter looks at how the iPad can be used as the best learning tool possible, meeting all kinds of educational demands. With access to digital textbooks and note-taking tools, it promotes particular uses like studying, writing, and critiquing essays. Through AAC apps and visual schedules, the iPad functions as an assistive communication device for kids who have trouble communicating. Additionally, puzzle games and brain-training apps can help older people develop their cognitive skills. The iPad is an effective tool for learners of all ages because of its adaptability, portability, and user-friendly interface.

The following chapter explores the world of digital healthcare, building on the iPad's many features. It looks at how the iPad may help people monitor their health and well-being by working with wearables and healthcare apps.

9

MONITORING HEALTH AND WELL-BEING USING DIGITAL HEALTHCARE

Find out how the iPad is revolutionizing healthcare settings. It digitalizes records and gives people the ability to keep track of their own health, revolutionizing the medical sector. Imagine your iPad serving as a customized, on-demand digital healthcare assistant. Discover its possibilities by investigating health-monitoring applications, taking vital signs, managing medicines, using telemedicine, and improving overall well-being. With its seamless integration, the iPad establishes itself as a crucial instrument for managing healthcare in the modern day and encourages people to take control of their health. Accept the enormous potential of your own iPad as you proceed through this stage of your journey towards healthcare.

APPS FOR MANAGING HEALTH AND OVERALL WELL-BEING

Apps for Fitness

Calorie Counter Apps: Apps that monitor calories are crucial tools for those who want to control their weight and eat a healthy diet. Apps like MyFitnessPal and Lose It! come highly recommended for keeping track of daily calorie intake and food intake. The App Store makes it simple to find and download these apps. Users may enter their meals and snacks in the applications, which will then provide nutritional data to assist them in selecting healthier foods.

Mental Health and Wellness Apps

I am

I am an app for mindfulness and meditation that provides guided meditation sessions for unwinding and lowering stress.

Better me

Another suggested app, BetterMe, offers tailored exercise programs and nutritious diet plans to assist users in achieving their fitness objectives.

Calm

An app called Calm promotes serenity and better sleep quality by providing guided meditations and calming bedtime stories.

These applications, which can be accessed and downloaded through the App Store, are all useful resources for improving mental health.

Sleep Apps

Apps for tracking sleep patterns and enhancing sleep quality are available. From the App Store, you may download suggested apps like Sleep Cycle, Headspace, or Meditation & Sleep. These applications track movement and sound while a user is sleeping using the iPad's sensors, giving users information about the quality of their sleep and the best times to get up. Understanding sleep patterns and establishing better sleep hygiene practices can help users.

Mood Tracking Apps

Users may track and record their feelings and moods with applications like Moodnotes and Daylio. You can obtain these apps from the App Store. Users who chronicle their daily moods, activities, and thoughts might see trends and learn more about their mental health. Apps that measure mood assist users in understanding their emotions and offer coping mechanisms for doing so.

Health Monitoring Apps

Apple's Health App

The iPad comes with a built-in function called Apple's Health App, which acts as a complete hub for health data. It gathers and organizes health data, including information on exercise, heart rate, sleep, and other elements. The Health App collects health information from a variety of sources, including linked devices, other health applications, and the iPad's sensors. Users may get all of their health information in one place.

Medications Tracker

Users may manage and keep track of their prescriptions and dose regimens with the assistance of applications like Medisafe and MyTherapy. You can obtain these apps from the App Store. To keep on top of their Medicine routine, users may create reminders, track adherence, and get notifications for refills. Apps that track drugs are especially useful for people who take several medications or have complicated dose regimens.

Step-by-Step Guide

Downloading an App

Open the App Store on your iPad and enter the app's name in the search bar to download it. To download the app, hit "Get" or the app's pricing after tapping it to discover more information about it. Enter your Apple ID password, or use Touch ID or Face ID for identification.

Wait as the iPad downloads and installs the software.

Opening or Accessing an App

Simply press an app's icon on the iPad's home screen to launch it after downloading it. Depending on your iPad's settings, apps are easily accessible from the home screen or app library.

Closing an App

For an app to be closed, swipe up from the bottom of the screen and stop in the center. Find the app you want to exit by swiping left or right, then swipe it up and off the screen. This action removes the app from the active state.

Uninstalling an App

The app icon on the home screen can be deleted by pressing and holding it until all the other icons start to wiggle. Once an app has been deleted, click "Install" after clicking the "X" in the top-left corner. After this action, the app is removed from your iPad.

Updating an App

If you've enabled this function in your iPad's settings, apps can update automatically. Open the App Store, choose your profile image in the upper right, and scroll down to check available updates to manually update an app. The app you wish to update has "Update" next to it. This guarantees that you are on the most recent version with enhanced features and bug fixes.

Navigating the App

Each program features a simple user interface with menus and buttons that are easy to find. Examine the app's settings and consult any available guides or tutorials to navigate it properly. The user-friendly design of the app makes it easy to access features like exercise regimens, nutrition planning, meditation programs, and sleep sounds.

Layout, Icons, and Other Features

Each app's layout and icons may be different, but they all generally have a clear and logical structure. Examples are calorie counter applications that show a list of foods and their accompanying calorie counts and meditation apps that provide a choice of guided meditation sessions. Through clearly identifiable menus and symbols, users may access functionality with ease.

Using All the basic and Unique Features

Explore and use each app's fundamental and distinctive features to get the most out of them. For instance, mental health applications may provide various meditation sessions for unwinding, concentrating, and sleeping. Utilize all of the features at your disposal to customize the app to your unique health requirements.

Troubleshoot Common Problems

Check for updates or get in touch with the app's support staff for assistance if you run into problems with it. Syncing failures, login problems, and small glitches are examples of common issues that may be fixed by updating the app or using troubleshooting instructions supplied by the app creators.

Pros and Cons

Personalized health management, simple recording of health measurements, and access to resources for enhancing general well-being are some advantages of these health and wellness applications. For full access to premium features, some applications may, nevertheless, demand memberships or in-app purchases. To see if an app fits within your budget and meets your health goals, take a look at its features and cost.

Price

Other health and wellness applications could require a one-time fee or membership for full use, while some provide free versions with restricted functions. Before making a choice, users should study the app's price information. For a more satisfying and healthy lifestyle, it may be useful to invest in applications that support your health and fitness objectives.

The extensive library of health and wellness apps for the iPad gives consumers the tools they need to take control of their health and enhance their general well-being. These applications address a range of health requirements, including exercise tracking, mental health assistance, sleep monitoring, and health data consolidation. Users may actively manage their health, make wise decisions, and adopt a better lifestyle by using these applications and learning about their capabilities. The iPad has undoubtedly transformed how people today manage and maintain their well-being by acting as a priceless digital healthcare assistant.

TIPS TO IMPROVE HEALTH AND WELL-BEING USING YOUR IPAD

Getting Healthy by Integrating the iPad With the Apple Watch

A robust health and fitness tracking system that combines the Apple Watch and iPad is possible. The iPad acts as a central repository for health data, while the Apple Watch is a wearable gadget that monitors several health parameters, including heart rate, exercise, and sleep. Users may track their fitness and health progress more effectively and obtain a full picture of their well-being by linking the Apple Watch with the iPad. Users must make sure their Apple Watch and iPad are Bluetooth paired and linked to the same Apple ID in order to activate this integration. On their iPad, customers may then open the Health app, touch on their profile image, choose "Health Profile," and add the Apple Watch as a device.

Managing Health Data on the iPad

Users may save, examine, and manage their health data in a single spot using the built-in Health app on the iPad. It compiles data from multiple sources, including linked gadgets, other health applications, and the Apple Watch. Users of the Health app may quickly view their health indicators, such as activity level, heart rate, sleep, and more, to help them decide what actions to take to improve their well-being. Users must find the Health app on their iPad's home screen, launch it, touch "Health Data" to access various health categories, and then personalize the dashboard to show the data that matters to them the most.

Sending Out Emergency Alerts on Dangerous Health Vitals, Especially for Seniors

For elders or anyone with special health issues, the iPad may be configured to send out emergency notifications in life-threatening circumstances. The iPad's Emergency SOS function enables users to communicate their position with emergency contacts while making a discrete request for assistance. When quick assistance is required due to serious health conditions or medical situations, this function adds an extra layer of protection and peace of mind.

Users must access "Settings" on their iPad, choose "Emergency SOS," and confirm that the "Call with Side Button" and "Auto Call" settings are turned on in order to activate the Emergency SOS function. Through the "Health" app, they may then add emergency contacts by visiting "Medical ID" and choosing "Edit" to include contacts.

Users may effectively monitor their health and make decisions about it by using these suggestions and the health and wellness tools on the iPad. Users may follow their progress and successfully work towards their fitness objectives thanks to the Apple Watch's interaction with the iPad, which offers a complete picture of health information. Users may easily access and manage their information thanks to the Health app, which serves as a single repository for health data.

The iPad's Emergency SOS function can be a lifeline for the elderly or others with certain health issues. It gives users the ability to ask for aid covertly in urgent situations and disclose their position to emergency contacts, ensuring prompt assistance. These suggestions make the iPad an invaluable tool for users of all ages by utilizing its features to enhance health and well-being.

SEGUE

The potential of the iPad as an effective tool for tracking one's health and fitness was covered in this chapter. Data management is made easier by the built-in Health app, and Emergency SOS adds essential security for emergencies. The iPad gives consumers the power to decide for themselves. We'll explore how the iPad transforms into the ideal travel companion in the following chapter, boosting the vacation experience with its portability and travel-related apps. The iPad redefines how consumers interact with technology for a richer life, just as it does for health and well-being, from itinerary planning to memory-keeping. Users are kept happy and in control of all elements of their lives by its versatility.

10

USING YOUR IPAD AS THE ULTIMATE TRAVEL COMPANION

APPS FOR TRAVELING, EXPLORING, AND GOING ON ADVENTURES

Traveling, exploring, and embarking on adventures are made effortless with the help of various apps available on the iPad. These apps cater to different aspects of travel, from navigation and translation to hotel bookings and food recommendations. Here, we will discuss each app or app category, including their purpose, features, step-by-step guides, pros and cons, and pricing.

Maps

Google Maps

- Google Maps is a well-known navigation tool that offers thorough maps, directions, real-time traffic updates, and information on public transportation.
- Best for scouting out and navigating uncharted territory.
- Features: Street View, offline maps, turn-by-turn directions, and location sharing
- Step-by-step instructions: The "Maps" app on iPads provides access to Google Maps, which is pre-installed on the device. Launch the app, enter your destination, and then adhere to the navigational prompts.
- Pros: Real-time traffic updates and accurate, current maps.
- Cons: Real-time navigation requires an internet connection.
- Cost: Free.

Google Earth

- Google Earth offers a 3D representation of the planet, enabling users to visit famous sites and locales all over the world.

- Function: Ideal for virtual travel and exploring new locations.
- 3D vision, interactive tours, and historical pictures are included.
- Step-by-step instructions: Get Google Earth from the App Store, launch it, and then look for a place you want to explore in 3D.
- Pros: Educational and immersive virtual exploration
- Cons: 3D imaging needs an internet connection.
- Cost: Free.

Directions

Waze

- Waze is a user-reported navigation app with a community focus that provides real-time traffic reports.
- Goal: Best for finding the quickest routes and avoiding traffic.
- Features: Users can report accidents and road closures, as well as real-time traffic warnings.
- Step-by-step instructions: To get real-time traffic updates, download Waze from the App Store, start the app, and enter your location.

- Pros: Reliable real-time traffic information that is community-driven.
- Cons: Limited offline functionality.
- Cost: Free.

Translation

Google Lens

- Text collected by the iPad's camera is translated and given information using image recognition technology provided by Google Lens.
- Use: Works best for instantaneous translation of foreign menus, signage, and text.
- Features: barcode scanning, object identification, and text translation.

- Detailed instructions: Google Lens is built into the Google app. Point the camera at the word or object you wish to translate or identify, then open the Google app and touch on the Lens icon.
- Pros: Text translation that is accurate and quick.
- Cons: The translation needs an internet connection.
- Cost: Free.

Google Translate

- Handwriting, speech, and text may all be translated using Google Translate, a language translation program.
- Use: The best tool for translating words and sentences between languages
- Features: offline language packs, speech translation, and text translation
- Step-by-step directions Then, start the app, choose the input and output languages, and then type or speak the text you want to translate. Download Google Translate from the App Store.
- Pros: Offline translation and extensive language support.

- Cons: For complicated phrases, machine translation is less accurate than human translation.
- Cost: Free.

Currency Converter

XE Currency App

- The currency converter app XE Currency offers real-time exchange rates for several currencies.
- Goal: Best for swift currency conversions for trip expenses
- Features: Offline mode, historical charts, and real-time exchange rates
- Step-by-step directions Open the XE Currency app after downloading it from the App Store, then enter the amount and the currencies you want to convert.
- Advantages: Current and accurate currency rates
- Cons: A subscription is required for some advanced functions.
- With in-app purchases for premium features, it is free.

Hotel Booking Apps

Airbnb app

- Airbnb is a website that enables customers to reserve distinctive lodging and experiences all around the world.
- Goal: Best for locating nearby and alternative lodgings
- Features: interactive map view, host reviews, and accommodation search
- Step-by-step instructions: download the Airbnb app from the App Store, register or log in, enter your travel dates and destination, and then browse the lodgings.
- Pros: A variety of distinctive lodging options
- Cons: The availability of some listings may be restricted.
- Cost: Downloading is free, but lodging costs vary.

Booking.com app

- A well-known website for booking hotels, Booking.com provides a variety of lodging choices and various reservation methods.
- Best for locating a range of hotel choices and comparing costs.

- Features include a wide range of lodging options, reviews from previous visitors, and flexible reservation terms.
- Step-by-step instructions: download Booking.com from the App Store, register or log in, choose your travel dates and destination, then look through the list of hotels.
- Pros: Numerous lodging selections and adaptable booking procedures
- Cons: Prices could change depending on inventory.
- Cost: Downloading is free, but lodging costs vary.

Transportation and Ride-Sharing Apps

Uber app

- Uber is a ride-sharing service that links passengers and drivers for easy transportation.
- Goal: The most effective way to locate on-demand transportation
- Features include fare estimations, driver tracking in real-time, and ride requests.
- Step-by-step instructions: get Uber from the App Store, register or log in, enter your destination, then make a ride request.

- Pros: Reliable and convenient transportation service
- Cons: Location-based availability may affect selection.
- Cost: Downloads are free; however, prices depend on demand and distance.

Lyft app

- A well-known ride-sharing app that offers similar services to Uber is Lyft.
- Goal: The best resource for discovering substitute ride-sharing services
- Features include fare estimations, driver tracking in real-time, and ride requests.
- Step-by-step instructions: get Lyft from the App Store, register or log in, enter your destination, then make a ride request.
- Competitive costs and a variety of riding alternatives are pros.
- Cons: In other places, coverage might not be as extensive.
- Cost: Downloads are free; however, prices depend on demand and distance.

Travel Planner Apps

TripCase app

- TripCase is a travel planner app that compiles travel details like flights, lodgings, and activities into a single itinerary.
- Goal: Ideal for planning and controlling travel schedules.
- Amenities: sharing of itineraries, hotel bookings, and flight monitoring
- Simple instructions: To construct an itinerary, download TripCase from the App Store, register or log in, and then enter your travel information.
- Real-time updates and centralized travel information are positives.
- Cons: A subscription may be needed for some functionality.
- With in-app purchases for premium features, it is free.

Hopper app

- Hopper is a travel app that enables users to search for and reserve the best hotel and airfare offers.
- Best for locating and monitoring flight pricing.

- Features: Hotel discounts, flight tracking, and price projections
- Step-by-step instructions: To get the best airfare and hotel deals, download Hopper from the App Store, register or log in, and then enter your travel information.
- Advantages: Predicting and tracking flight prices
- Cons: Only available for hotel and airline reservations.
- Cost: Downloading is free; however, lodging and travel costs can differ.

Culture Trip App

- For a variety of locations, Culture Trip provides city tours and individualized travel advice.
- Best for learning about local culture and sights.
- Features: travel articles, tailored recommendations, and curated city guides
- How-to: Download Culture Trip from the App Store, register or log in, then peruse city guides and recommendations tailored to you.
- Pros: Travelers can access curated and educational content.
- Cons: Only available in city directories and suggestions.

- Cost: There is no charge to download.

Food and Restaurant Apps

Yelp app

- Yelp is a restaurant review software that aids users in discovering and perusing nearby eateries and establishments.
- Goal: Excellent for reading reviews and finding new places.
- Features: user reviews, photographs, and restaurant search.
- Install Yelp from the App Store, register or log in, and then use the location and cuisine filters to find restaurants.
- Pros: Comprehensive ratings and reviews of restaurants.
- Cons: It's possible that certain eateries lack reviews.
- Cost: There is no charge to download.

Uber Eats app

- Uber Eats is a meal delivery service that enables customers to place takeout or delivery orders for food from nearby restaurants.
- Goal: Best for on-the-go food orders

- Features include delivery tracking, menu browsing, and restaurant search.
- Step-by-step directions Install the Uber Eats app from the App Store, create an account or log in, and then look up restaurants and food items to order.
- A convenient food delivery service is a pro.
- Cons: The availability of delivery services may vary by location.
- Cost: Downloading is free; however, food costs and delivery costs vary.

Zomato

- Zomato is an app for finding restaurants and ordering food that offers restaurant lists and reviews from customers.
- Goal: Ideal for discovering nearby eateries and dining options.
- Features: ordering food, user reviews, and restaurant search.
- How-to: Install Zomato from the App Store, register or log in, and browse restaurant listings and user ratings.
- Advantages: Numerous dining alternatives and user-generated content

- Cons: The availability of delivery services may vary by location.
- Cost: Downloading is free; however, food costs and delivery costs vary.

TIPS TO MAXIMIZE THE IPAD AS THE ULTIMATE TRAVEL BUDDY

iPad Settings for Travel

- Changing iPad settings for best travel use, including data roaming and offline functionality,
- Purpose: To monitor data use, minimize unexpected charges, and provide offline access to critical apps and content.
- To enable data roaming, navigate to Settings > Cellular Data > Data Roaming. To enable or stop data roaming, toggle the switch.
- Offline Entertainment: Download movies, TV shows, and music from streaming services such as Netflix and Apple Music for offline viewing while traveling.

Protecting Your Personal Data From Public Wi-Fi and Hotspots

- Using security precautions to protect personal information when connecting to public Wi-Fi networks and hotspots
- Purpose: To guard against data breaches and unauthorized access to sensitive information.
- Invest in a Virtual Private Network (VPN): Install a trustworthy VPN program from the program Store, such as ExpressVPN. To encrypt data, activate the VPN before connecting to public Wi-Fi.

Using AirTags to Track Belongings

Using Apple's AirTag to track and locate misplaced items while traveling

- Purpose: To keep track of valuable objects such as bags, backpacks, or cameras.
- Securely attach an AirTag to your items.
- Use the Find My app: On your iPad, launch the Find My app to track the location of your belongings.

Using eSIM

Using an electronic SIM (eSIM) on an iPad to gain easy overseas data access

- Purpose: To avoid physically swapping SIM cards and to use local data plans when abroad.
- Enable eSIM: Navigate to Settings > Cellular Data, and then Add a Cellular Plan. Set up your eSIM by following the on-screen instructions.

Discover and use these applications and tricks while traveling to make the most of your iPad. Your iPad may become the ideal travel companion by letting you easily explore, discover, and enjoy your adventure with the correct apps and settings.

SEGUE

This chapter focused on the world of travel applications that turn the iPad into the ideal trip companion. We looked at a variety of travel-related apps, including everything from directions and translation to hotel reservations and eating advice. Waze and Google Maps made navigation simple, and Google Translate and Google Lens made language conversion easier. XE Currency streamlined currency transactions, while Booking.com and Airbnb provided a variety of lodging choices. To help readers make wise decisions, step-by-step instructions, a list of benefits and drawbacks, and price information were provided.

Looking ahead to the next chapter, we'll investigate the fascinating opportunities for fusing the iPad with other Apple products to create a seamless, linked experience. We will explore the power of Apple device synergy, from AirDrop for simple file sharing to Handoff for smooth device switching. Continuity capabilities like Continuity Camera and Continuity Sketch will also create new opportunities for innovation and productivity. The chapter will offer detailed instructions on how to activate and make use of these integrations, ensuring that readers get the most out of their Apple ecosystem. With a thorough understanding of how to connect your iPad with other Apple devices, embrace the future of technology.

11

INTEGRATING YOUR IPAD WITH OTHER APPLE GEAR

Discover the hidden hardware wonders from Apple that some iPad customers aren't aware of. Have you ever wanted a quick way to transfer files between iPads? Did you know that there's more to meeting other iPad users than just online chatting? Taking advantage of the iPad's flexibility in productivity, creativity, and fun, Apple has created a number of capabilities that enable seamless networking and collaboration. This comprehensive tutorial will look at these unique Apple gears and arm you with clear instructions for utilizing them, as well as troubleshooting suggestions to ensure your experience is trouble-free. Prepare to take full advantage of your iPad-to-iPad connections.

AirDrop

A wireless file-sharing function called AirDrop enables users to quickly move documents, videos, and other data between Apple devices, including iPads, that are close by. Removes the need to share files through wires, emails, or messaging apps. It establishes a direct peer-to-peer connection between devices using a combination of Wi-Fi and Bluetooth technology for rapid and discreet transfers.

Step-by-step guide on how to enable or use it

1. Turn on Bluetooth and Wi-Fi on both devices.
2. To access the Control Center, swipe down from the sending iPad's top-right corner.
3. To enlarge the "Network Settings" box, press and hold it in the top-left area of the Control Center.
4. Choose whether you want to limit access to contacts exclusively or to everyone by tapping "AirDrop."
5. Verify that AirDrop is enabled on the receiving iPad by following the same instructions.
6. After choosing a file, picture, or document, hit the "Share" button.
7. Find the receiving iPad's symbol in the AirDrop portion of the sharing choices and press it.

8. After accepting the file, the transfer will start after the receiver is prompted to do so.

Troubleshooting problems

- Check that Wi-Fi and Bluetooth are both turned on and that both devices are in close proximity to one another if AirDrop is unable to connect two devices.
- Restart both devices and give AirDrop another shot if it's not working. Occasionally, connectivity issues may be resolved by a simple restart.

Handoff

With the help of the Handoff feature, users can start a task on one Apple device and continue it on another without interruption, enabling seamless switching between several Apple devices. Through handoff, Apple products provide a seamless user experience that encourages continuity and productivity. You might begin composing an email on your iPad and finish it on your iPhone, for instance.

Step-by-step guide on how to enable or use it

1. Check to see whether Bluetooth is enabled, if both devices are connected to the same Wi-Fi network, and if they are both logged in with the same Apple ID.
2. Start the task you want to transfer on the sending iPad (such as writing an email or browsing the web).
3. On the receiving iPad, check the App Switcher or the Lock Screen's lower-left corner for the app's icon.
4. Tap the app's icon to complete the task without interruption on the receiving device.

Troubleshooting problems

If Handoff is not working, ensure both devices meet the requirements stated above (same Apple ID, Wi-Fi, and Bluetooth). Also, verify that Handoff is enabled on both devices in Settings > General > AirPlay & Handoff > Handoff.

Continuity

The features that make it possible for interactions between Apple devices to go smoothly include Handoff, Instant Hotspot, Universal Clipboard, and others. Through the promotion of continuity, an environment where devices interact well together is created, resulting in a fluid user experience that lets people work across different devices.

Step-by-step guide on how to enable or use it

1. Check to see if Bluetooth is active and that each of the linked devices is utilizing the same Apple ID and connected to the same Wi-Fi network.
2. Select the option to take a photo or scan a document with your iPad by clicking on the relevant location within a supported app on your Mac.
3. To use Continuity Markup, select "Markup" from the document or image preview menu on your iPad. The selected item will then appear for annotation on your Mac.
4. Create a new email or note on your Mac, then select the Markup icon to use Continuity Sketch. Choose "iPad" to use your iPad to do sketches or add annotations.
5. Make sure Instant Hotspot is turned on on your iPhone by going to Settings > Cellular > Personal Hotspot. Select "Personal Hotspot" from the drop-down menu under Settings > Wi-Fi on your iPad to establish a connection.
6. In order to use Universal Clipboard, be certain that both devices are logged in with the same

Apple ID and are linked to the same Wi-Fi network. You can transfer content from one device to another by using the standard copy-and-paste commands.

Troubleshooting problems

If Continuity features are not working, ensure both devices meet the requirements stated above (same Apple ID, Wi-Fi, and Bluetooth). Also, verify that Handoff is enabled on both devices in Settings > General > AirPlay & Handoff > Handoff.

Auto Unlock

Users can utilize Touch ID or Face ID authentication on their iPad or iPhone to automatically unlock their Mac by utilizing the Auto Unlock function. By using the user's trusted Apple devices for authentication, Auto Unlock simplifies, secures, and improves the login process.

Step-by-step guide on how to enable or use it

1. Ensure that two-factor authentication is activated and that the same Apple ID is used to sign in on both devices.
2. Select System Preferences > Security & Privacy > General on your Mac.

3. Verify that "Use your Apple Watch to unlock apps and your Mac" is turned on and select the checkbox for "Allow your Apple Watch to unlock your Mac."

4. If Auto Unlock is configured, your Mac will automatically unlock when you wake it from sleep if your iPad or iPhone is nearby and unlocked.

Troubleshooting problems

If Auto Unlock is not working, ensure both devices meet the requirements stated above (two-factor authentication, same Apple ID). Make sure your Mac and iPad/iPhone are running the latest software updates.

Instant Hotspot

When Wi-Fi is not available, the iPad can use Instant Hotspot to connect to the internet using the cellular connection of an iPhone nearby. With the help of Instant Hotspot, iPad users can connect to the internet while on the road, even if they don't have a specific iPad cellular plan.

Step-by-step guide on how to enable or use it

1. Ensure Bluetooth and Personal Hotspot are turned on and that both devices are logged in with the same Apple ID.
2. On your iPad, select Settings > Wi-Fi and check for the name of your iPhone under "Personal Hotspot."
3. After choosing your iPhone, the iPad will instantly establish an internet connection via its cellular network.

Troubleshooting problems (if applicable):

If Instant Hotspot is not working, ensure both devices meet the requirements stated above (same Apple ID, Wi-Fi, and Bluetooth). Make sure Personal Hotspot is turned on under Settings > Cellular > Personal Hotspot on your iPhone.

Sidecar

Sidecar allows users to extend their Mac desktop to their iPad and use it as a second display or a drawing tablet with Apple Pencil support. Sidecar enhances productivity and creativity by providing a larger canvas for multitasking or drawing directly on supported apps.

Step-by-step guide on how to enable or use it:

1. Ensure both devices are signed in with the same Apple ID and connected via Bluetooth and the same Wi-Fi network.
2. On your Mac, pick your iPad under "Connect to" by clicking the AirPlay symbol in the menu bar.
3. Alternatively, go to System Preferences > Sidecar and choose your iPad from the dropdown menu.
4. Your iPad will now extend your Mac's display, allowing you to use it as a second monitor.

Troubleshooting problems

If Sidecar is not working, ensure both devices meet the requirements stated above (same Apple ID, Wi-Fi, and Bluetooth). Check that Sidecar is enabled on your Mac in System Preferences > Sidecar.

Universal Clipboard

Multiple Apple devices connected to the same Apple ID can seamlessly copy and paste using the Universal Clipboard. By enabling users to copy content from one device and paste it on another without the assistance of a third party, Universal Clipboard streamlines the process of sharing content between devices.

Step-by-step guide on how to enable or use it

1. Make sure that the same Apple ID is used to log into both devices and that they are both linked to the same Wi-Fi network.
2. Text, pictures, or documents can all be copied to one device.
3. Tap and hold the spot on the other device where you wish to paste the material.
4. After selecting it, the option to paste from the Universal Clipboard will show up, and the material will be pasted.

Troubleshooting problems

Make sure both devices satisfy the prerequisites listed above (same Apple ID, Wi-Fi) if Universal Clipboard isn't functioning. Additionally, confirm that Handoff is turned on in Settings > General > AirPlay & Handoff > Handoff on both devices.

Universal Control

With the impending Universal Control feature in macOS Monterey, users will be able to drag and drop items between various Apple devices with ease. When utilizing numerous Apple devices at once, Universal Control offers an even more fluid experience, boosting productivity and teamwork.

A step-by-step guide on how to enable and use Universal Control

1. To ensure compatibility with Universal Control, update your Mac and iPad to macOS Monterey and iPadOS 15 or later, respectively.
2. Verify that the same Apple ID is used to sign in on both devices and that they are both linked to the same Wi-Fi network.
3. Place your iPad next to your Mac. The smooth operation of Universal Control requires physical proximity.
4. Open System Preferences on your Mac.
5. Select "Displays."
6. Choose the "Arrangement" tab.
7. The "Arrangement" option will now be shown at the bottom of the window. Drag and drop the iPad icon into the desired location on your Mac's display.
8. To make it easier to access the Universal Control menu, enable the "Show displays in the menu bar" option.
9. Check that Handoff is turned on in Settings > General > AirPlay & Handoff > Handoff on your iPad.

Troubleshooting problems

Verify that both devices are running macOS Monterey and iPadOS 15 or newer if Universal Control isn't functioning. Assume both devices are logged in with the same Apple ID, connected to the same Wi-Fi network, and that Handoff is enabled on your iPad. Any connectivity issues could be resolved by restarting both devices.

iCloud

Apple's cloud-based storage and syncing service, known as iCloud, enables customers to sync and store data from all of their Apple devices, including backups, images, and documents. iCloud gives consumers access to their information from anywhere by offering a seamless solution to keep files and data current and accessible across all Apple devices.

Step-by-step guide on how to enable or use it

1. Verify that the same Apple ID is used to sign in on all devices.
2. Navigate to Settings > [Your Name] > iCloud on each device.
3. Turn on the relevant iCloud services, such as iCloud Drive and iCloud Photos, that you want to use.

4. Now, your files and images across all of your Apple devices will sync automatically.

Troubleshooting problems

Make sure all devices are online and logged in with the same Apple ID if iCloud isn't successfully synchronizing. Check that iCloud services are enabled in Settings > [Your Name] > iCloud.

iCloud Drive

The file storage portion of iCloud, known as iCloud Drive, enables users to store files and retrieve them from any Apple device. By offering a central home for all files and keeping them accessible and current across Apple devices, iCloud Drive streamlines file management.

Step-by-step guide on how to enable or use it

1. Verify that iCloud Drive is activated as instructed in the preceding step.
2. To access iCloud Drive on your iPad, use the Files app.
3. You can find "iCloud Drive" by selecting "Locations" from the menu at the bottom of the screen after selecting "Browse."

4. Select iCloud Drive from the menu to view and manage your files.

Troubleshooting problems

If iCloud Drive is not syncing or showing all files, ensure your devices are connected to the internet and signed in with the same Apple ID. Also, check that iCloud Drive is enabled in Settings > [Your Name] > iCloud.

iCloud Photos

Across all Apple devices, iCloud Photos automatically stores and syncs pictures and videos. All of your images and videos are automatically backed up by iCloud and are accessible on all of your Apple devices, conserving storage space and giving you peace of mind.

Step-by-step guide on how to enable or use it

1. Verify that iCloud Photos is activated as instructed in the preceding section.
2. The iPad's Photos app should be opened.
3. Tap "Photos" at the bottom of the screen to access your photos and videos.

Troubleshooting problems

If iCloud Photos is not syncing or showing all photos, ensure your devices are connected to the internet and signed in with the same Apple ID. Also, check that iCloud Photos is enabled in Settings > [Your Name] > iCloud > Photos.

Apple Music

Users of the music streaming service Apple Music have on-demand access to a huge library of songs, playlists, and albums. With Apple Music, consumers can browse selected material based on their interests and listening history, create playlists, and listen to a variety of music.

Step-by-step guide on how to enable or use it:

1. Start the iPad's Apple Music app.
2. Use your Apple ID to log in, or create one if you don't already have one.
3. Look through or perform a search for tunes, performers, albums, or playlists.
4. Tap any piece of content to start the music playing.

Troubleshooting problems

If Apple Music is not working, check your internet connection and ensure you are signed in with a valid

Apple ID. Also, if you are a paid user, make sure that your Apple Music subscription is active.

Apple TV+

The premium streaming service from Apple, known as Apple TV+, features original TV series, films, documentaries, and other content. On their iPad and other Apple devices, customers can watch premium, exclusive content through Apple TV+, putting entertainment at their fingertips.

Step-by-step guide on how to enable or use it

1. On your iPad, launch the Apple TV app.
2. Log in with your Apple ID, or create one if you don't already have one.
3. Look through the content that is accessible and tap on any episode or movie to start watching.

Troubleshooting problems

If Apple TV+ is not working, check your internet connection and ensure you are signed in with a valid Apple ID. Also, ensure that your Apple TV+ subscription is active if you are a paying subscriber.

AirPlay

Using the AirPlay function, users can wirelessly broadcast audio, video, and photos from an iPad or iPhone to an Apple TV or other AirPlay-compatible devices. By enabling users to view material from their iPad on a bigger screen, such as a TV, or play audio on compatible speakers, AirPlay improves enjoyment.

Step-by-step guide on how to enable or use it

1. Ensure that the iPad is linked to the same Wi-Fi network as the AirPlay-capable device (such as the Apple TV).
2. Open the app on your iPad that contains the media you want to AirPlay, such as Photos, Videos, or Music.
3. Select the AirPlay icon, which is typically found in the Share menu or the playback controls.
4. To begin streaming, choose an AirPlay-capable device from the list.

Troubleshooting problems

If AirPlay is not working, ensure both devices are connected to the same Wi-Fi network. Restart both devices if needed, as this can often resolve connectivity issues.

Apple Pay

Using their iPad or iPhone, customers may utilize Apple Pay to make safe transactions in stores, online, and within apps. Apple Pay offers a safe and practical alternative to using physical credit or debit cards for payment processing.

Step-by-step guide on how to enable or use it:

1. Navigate to Settings > Wallet & Apple Pay on your iPad.
2. Tap "Add Card" to add a credit or debit card to Apple Pay.
3. Follow the on-screen instructions to validate the card and complete the setup.
4. Double-click the side button or home button on your iPad when requested to authenticate using Face ID or Touch ID in order to utilize Apple Pay in stores. To complete the transaction, hold your iPad close to the payment machine.

Troubleshooting problems

If Apple Pay is not working, ensure your iPad supports Apple Pay and has a supported payment card added. Also, make sure you've enabled Face ID or Touch ID for authentication.

Text Message Forwarding

Users of the iPad can send and receive SMS and MMS messages from their iPhones on their iPad thanks to text message forwarding. With text message forwarding, it's simple to keep in touch and reply to texts from your iPad without taking out your iPhone.

Step-by-step guide on how to enable or use it:

1. Ensure that your iPad and iPhone are both connected to the same Wi-Fi network and are both signed in with the same Apple ID.
2. On your iPhone, go to Settings > Messages > Text Message Forwarding.
3. Turn on the switch next to your iPad in the list of devices.
4. To complete the configuration, your iPad will receive a code that must be entered on your iPhone.
5. After you've configured everything, you can use your iPad's Messages app to send and receive SMS and MMS messages.

Troubleshooting problems

If Text Message Forwarding is not working, ensure both devices meet the requirements stated above (same

Apple ID, Wi-Fi). Restart both devices if needed, as this can often resolve connectivity issues.

SEGUE

The chapter looks at different Apple devices that enable iPad-to-iPad communication and improve user experiences. File sharing, multitasking, and device switching are made easier by features like AirDrop, Handoff, and Continuity. The productivity-enhancing features are Auto Unlock, Instant Hotspot, and Universal Clipboard. Additionally, Apple Music, Apple TV+, and AirPlay enhance entertainment, and iCloud promotes easy data syncing between devices. Text Message Forwarding improves communication. The chapter offers step-by-step instructions and troubleshooting advice. The following chapter, "Preparing for the Future: Tips for Adapting to Evolving iPad Capabilities," teaches users how to use these capabilities efficiently, adjust to changing iPad technology, and remain current with new developments to make the most of their iPad usage.

12

PREPARING FOR THE FUTURE— TIPS FOR ADAPTING TO EVOLVING IPAD CAPABILITIES

In this chapter, we examine the fast-changing environment of iPad features and apps, providing readers with tips on how to prepare for the future. iPads are only one personal device that demonstrates how swiftly technology is evolving. We reassure readers that this book is their roadmap for embracing the future with confidence, despite concerns about needing to learn new layouts and intricate features. By supplying readers with knowledge and skills, we enable them to take full advantage of cutting-edge technologies and adapt to impending developments without difficulty. Making sure readers can easily manage the flow of new iPad features is the goal in order to fully utilize these cutting-edge technologies.

FUTURE TRENDS IN APPLE TECHNOLOGY AND WHAT THIS MEANS FOR THE IPAD

Apple has led the way in innovation in the ever-evolving world of technology, continuously pushing the boundaries and establishing benchmarks for the industry. The appearance of iPads and the experience for iPad users will surely change significantly as Apple continues to adopt and incorporate cutting-edge technologies. In this thorough research, we will examine upcoming developments in Apple technology and how they will affect the iPad.

Augmented Reality (AR) and Virtual Reality (VR)

Virtual and augmented reality have become very popular and have many practical applications. Users can anticipate immersive AR experiences that mix digital information with the actual environment when they are integrated into the iPad. On the other side, VR capabilities can whisk users away to virtual worlds, enhancing the appeal of entertainment, training, and gaming.

The way people engage with the material on their iPads will be completely transformed by AR and VR. The possibilities range from augmented reality (AR) shopping experiences to virtual reality (VR) trip tours. Users can anticipate a more enriched and engrossing user experience that blends the real and virtual worlds.

Users may need to become familiar with AR development frameworks, 3D modeling, and VR content creation tools in order to fully utilize AR and VR on iPads. It will be useful to know how to adapt user experiences to various screen sizes and devices.

Learning AR and VR might be a little difficult, especially for people who are just getting started with 3D modeling and development. However, there are a ton of tutorials and online tools that might make learning easier.

To get a feel for the technology, start with straightforward AR and VR activities. Develop AR apps with SwiftUI and ARKit, and create VR content using Unity and other platforms. Participating in online forums and attending workshops can also help one better comprehend these technologies.

Artificial Intelligence (AI) and Machine Learning (ML)

iPads will be able to carry out increasingly complex activities thanks to AI and ML, including intelligent automation, natural language processing, and personalized content recommendations.

More intuitive and individualized user experiences on iPads will result from the integration of AI and ML. Devices will adjust to user preferences, improving the effectiveness of tasks like searching, organizing, and content recommendations.

Users may need to comprehend the foundations of AI algorithms, data analysis, and ML models in order to benefit from AI and ML on iPads. It will be advantageous to have knowledge of programming languages like Python.

The intricacy of AI and ML makes learning them difficult. Both beginning and advanced learners can find a variety of online materials and courses to help them understand the ideas.

Utilize TensorFlow and Scikit-Learn frameworks, to begin with easy machine-learning tasks. To obtain practical experience, take part in online AI challenges and Kaggle tournaments. Insights can also be gained by following AI authorities and going to industry conferences.

5G Connectivity

The total network performance on iPads will improve thanks to 5G connectivity's lightning-fast data transfer and dramatically reduced latency.

Users can anticipate quicker upload and download speeds, snag-free video streaming, and enhanced app performance. Online gaming and real-time applications will both be more responsive as a result of the decreased latency.

Users will benefit from knowing the technical details of 5G networks and how they differ from earlier generations, so they can take full advantage of this technology.

As learning about 5G requires comprehending cellular networks and their evolution, it can be a little difficult. But there are online tools and articles that make the ideas simpler.

Keep up with the latest 5G developments and where it is being used. Try out 5G-enabled apps and services to see the enhanced performance for yourself.

Wearables and Health Technology

Apple Watch and other wearable devices will continue to sync data with iPads without any issues, allowing for more thorough health and fitness tracking.

As health information from wearables is effortlessly linked with iPads, users will experience Apple products more holistically. The iPad has the potential to develop into a hub for health-related knowledge.

The Apple Watch's or other wearables' features and capabilities, as well as how to interpret and use health data, may need to be familiarized users.

Apple's flawless device integration makes it relatively simple to learn how to use wearables with iPads. Research may be necessary to fully comprehend the health data and its implications.

For optimum compatibility, make sure that both the Apple Watch and iPad are using the most recent software. To make the most of their combined functionalities, familiarize yourself with the health apps and settings on both devices.

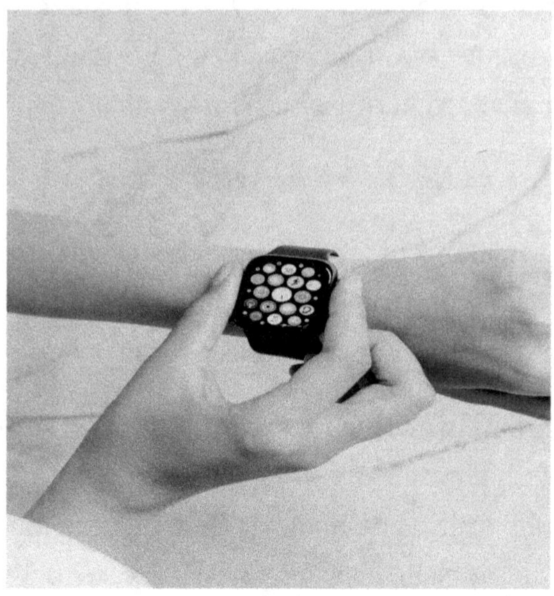

Foldable Devices

Larger displays that can be folded for portability are anticipated for foldable devices. The iPad might experiment with flexible form factors for more screen space.

Users using foldable iPads will have access to larger displays when necessary and portable storage when traveling. More flexibility for multitasking and content consumption is provided by this.

Users may need to learn new navigation and multitasking techniques that are unique to the foldable form factor in order to become accustomed to foldable smartphones.

Due to the unusual interaction methods, using foldable devices may be difficult at first, but with repeated use, users should get used to the new user experience.

Try out foldable technology to get a feel for its capabilities and applications. Watch for updates from Apple regarding the anticipated availability of foldable iPads in the future.

Digital Payments and Fintech

As digital payment methods like Apple Pay advance, iPad purchases will become more secure and easy.

Users may pay more swiftly and easily with the iPad, whether in-person or online. Peace of mind throughout transactions will be offered by enhanced security features.

Users must become familiar with the configuration and security options of online payment services like Apple Pay.

In general, using digital payment services is simple because they come with detailed setup instructions.

Install digital payment methods on your iPad, then look into different merchants and apps that support them. Use security best practices to safeguard your financial data.

Voice-First Interactions

Users will increasingly be able to engage with their iPads using natural language commands thanks to voice-first interactions.

On their iPads, users can perform tasks, conduct informational searches, and manage apps hands-free by using voice commands.

It will be useful to master voice commands for different tasks and how to use voice assistants like Siri successfully.

Due to their user-friendly design, voice assistants and voice commands are typically simple to learn how to use.

Try out Siri on your iPad for different tasks and learn about the variety of voice commands that are available. Keep current with voice recognition technology updates and new features.

Swift 6

The most recent version of Apple's programming language, Swift 6, will provide better performance and additional features for creating iPad apps.

Swift 6 will let developers construct iPad apps that are more effective and powerful, resulting in slicker and quicker user experiences.

Learning Swift 6's new features and grammar will be crucial for developers if they want to get the most out of the language.

The developer's familiarity with Swift's earlier iterations will determine how easily they pick up Swift 6. It could take some time for beginners to fully understand the ideas.

Keep up with Apple's developer resources, and check out Swift 6 presentations at WWDC to learn about the most recent updates and best practices.

iBeacon Trends

iPads will be able to communicate with neighboring Bluetooth Low Energy (BLE) devices thanks to iBeacon technology, enabling location-based experiences.

Users of iBeacon can anticipate contextually aware and tailored experiences based on their actual location.

Developers might need to grasp BLE technology and how to include iBeacon features into their apps in order to benefit from iBeacon trends.

It can be relatively difficult to learn how to use iBeacon technology, especially for developers who are unfamiliar with BLE ideas.

To learn about the potential uses of iBeacon technology, investigate the apps and experiences that use it. For advice on how to incorporate iBeacon technology, consult Apple's instructions.

Wireless Charging

When charging iPads, wireless charging will replace the need for wired connections, improving portability and convenience.

Users may use their iPads more freely while charging, thanks to the cable-free charging experience.

Since wireless charging will be a common function built into upcoming iPad models, no special knowledge is required to use it.

It only takes putting the iPad down on a suitable wireless charging station for wireless charging to work.

To ensure optimum performance, spend money on a reliable wireless charging pad that supports the iPad's charging specifications.

Blockchain

Blockchain technology might be used for iPad digital asset management and safe data storage.

On iPads, users can benefit from improved security and privacy for their data and transactions, lowering the likelihood of data breaches.

Users might need to become familiar with blockchain technology and the possible applications for iPads.

Learning about blockchain and its uses can be a little difficult, especially for individuals who are unfamiliar with decentralized technologies.

Investigate blockchain-based software and services to learn how the technology actually functions. Keep up with changes in the blockchain integration business.

The design of iPads and the user experience for iPad users will change significantly as Apple adopts these upcoming trends. Users should become familiar with the particular knowledge and abilities required for each trend in order to adapt to and fully benefit from these technologies. Even if some technologies could present mild difficulties, the quantity of internet information and courses will help users navigate these recent developments without worry. Users may confidently embrace the future of Apple technology and improve their iPad experiences by being curious, investigating useful applications, and participating in online communities.

Share the Knowledge!

It is my hope that you're going to get so much more out of your iPad than you realized you could – and now you're in a great position to help other users do the same.

Simply by sharing your honest opinion of this book and a little about your own experience, you'll show new readers where they can find all the guidance they need to access the full potential of their iPad.

Thanks so much for your support. Enjoy your device!

Scan the QR code below

CONCLUSION

The power and potential of the iPad have been thoroughly examined in this extensive book, revealing how users of all ages and educational levels may take advantage of all of its features. The most important lesson is to embrace the iPad's adaptability and potential, changing it from a basic gadget into a potent tool that improves communication, productivity, creativity, entertainment, and leisure.

Understanding the various iPad models and their distinctive characteristics was the first step in the quest. We discovered that each iPad serves a certain function, from the 12.9-inch and 11-inch iPad Pro models created for professionals and creatives to the iPad Air and standard iPad models suitable for casual users and students. With this information in hand, readers may make an informed decision regarding which iPad model best suits their needs.

We concentrated on improving the iPad's usability and accessibility for seniors in the chapter on senior-friendly iPad features. We make sure that the iPad can be used easily by people of all abilities by tweaking settings for visual, hearing, and mobility problems, such as changing font size, turning on voice control, and utilizing accessibility features. In order to ensure an inclusive experience, we also looked into assistive technology and apps made specifically for elders.

Data security plays an important role in today's digital world; therefore, we placed special emphasis on protecting iPad data from internet threats like viruses and phishing scams. We talked about the significance of two-factor authentication and iCloud Private Relay, as well as fundamental security techniques, including data encryption, biometrics, and passcodes. Users may navigate the digital world with confidence by following safe surfing practices and controlling app permissions.

A wide range of essential accessories can greatly enhance the iPad experience. We provide comprehensive guidance on how to choose dependable protective cases and coverings for the iPad from brands like OtterBox, Speck, and Apple Smart Cover/Smart Folio. We suggested keyboard cases that turn the iPad into a laptop-like tool for professionals and academics. Noise-canceling headphones from Sony, Bose, and Apple AirPods Pro were recommended for immersive listening, while portable Bluetooth speakers were recommended for outdoor enthusiasts and social events. Lightning Cables allowed for data syncing and charging, while USB-C Power Adapters allowed for fast charging.

In the chapter on productivity suggestions, the iPad's tremendous possibilities for both business and personal tasks were tapped. To boost productivity, we focused on multitasking, setting customization, and the usage of tools like Split View and Slide Over. Users may maximize their time and work more productively by optimizing workflows, communicating with photos using Live Text, and maximizing Safari browsing through extensions. Focus Mode lets users handle their vital work easily by reducing interruptions and aiding in task prioritization.

We looked at how the iPad may be set up and optimized for immersive entertainment. The iPad becomes a mobile entertainment center when it comes to configuring streaming services like Netflix, HBO Go, and Disney+ for movies and TV series, as well as listening to music through iTunes and Spotify. On social media sites like YouTube, TikTok, and Snapchat, short films and user-generated material provide countless opportunities for creativity and entertainment. The App Store offers a wide variety of games for players to enjoy. The iPad goes beyond being a tool for productivity and becomes a center for engaging entertainment.

Communication goes beyond entertainment, and the iPad creates new opportunities for interpersonal interaction. This chapter examined communication-related iPad apps, such as messaging, video calling, and social media sites. Users can engage with friends and browse a variety of material with the help of apps like Facebook, Twitter, Instagram, Clubhouse, Reddit, Pinterest, and LinkedIn. Connecting with friends, family, and coworkers is simple with the help of messaging and video calling apps like FaceTime, Telegram, WhatsApp, Messenger, Mail, Gmail, Google Meet, Skype, Zoom, and Discord. Reliable phone calls and text messaging are provided via built-in messaging and call apps like Messages and Calls.

The iPad is a standout learning tool in the educational space, meeting a range of educational needs. The iPad aids students of all ages, enabling them to access digital textbooks, take notes, and critique writings, as well as serve as an AAC device and visual timetable for children who have communication difficulties. Puzzle games and brain-training apps help seniors improve their cognitive abilities. The iPad transforms into a powerful tool for lifelong learning and individual development because of its versatility, portability, and user-friendly design.

The iPad's potential to monitor health and well-being by integrating with wearables and healthcare apps was studied in the chapter on digital healthcare. Data management is made easier by the built-in Health app, and emergency security is increased with Emergency SOS. With access to a variety of fitness and health apps that let users make educated decisions about their well-being, the iPad gives users the power to take control of their health. Users can reach their health objectives and maintain awareness of their well-being with the iPad as a health companion.

The iPad is the perfect travel companion, making travel more fun and easy. The iPad makes traveling a breeze, from navigating with apps like Waze and Google Maps to interpreting languages using Google Lens and Google Translate. Converting currencies is made simple by XE Currency, and there are many housing options available through applications like Booking.com and Airbnb. Readers can confidently make the most of their vacation experience with the iPad by their side thanks to step-by-step instructions and insights into the best apps.

When the iPad is combined with other Apple products, its power soars to new heights. The user experience is enhanced by features like AirDrop for simple file sharing, Handoff for seamless device switching, and Continuity Camera and Continuity Sketch for creativity and productivity. Apple Music, Apple TV+, and AirPlay provide endless entertainment, while Auto Unlock, Instant Hotspot, and Universal Clipboard increase productivity. The connection between devices is improved via Text Message Forwarding, while data synchronization is simplified by iCloud. This chapter equips readers to make the most of their Apple ecosystem by offering detailed instructions and troubleshooting guidance.

The final chapters emphasize getting ready for emerging iPad trends and technology. Users can adopt new features and functions by keeping up with evolving technologies like augmented reality, artificial intelligence, 5G connections, wearables, and digital payments. By being aware of these trends, users may utilize the iPad's full capabilities and maintain an edge in the rapidly changing digital environment.

Your iPad is more than just a gadget; it's your best friend in the rapidly evolving digital space. Accept the opportunities, open up new vistas, follow your passions, and stay in touch with your loved ones. The iPad improves every part of your life, from business and school to leisure and communication, thanks to its adaptability, user-friendly design, and wide selection of apps.

Please leave a review and share your thoughts if you've found our complete guide on using an iPad to be incredibly useful and user-friendly to help others decide if this book is the appropriate one for them. Your advice will be incredibly helpful in assisting others in maximizing the potential of their iPad.

I genuinely hope that this guide has given you the tools you need to effectively utilize your iPad and all of its features. I appreciate you joining me on this adventure, and I hope your iPad explorations bring you countless hours of happiness and contentment. May your iPad become your go-to device in the constantly expanding digital space.

GLOSSARY

Adware: Is software that displays unwanted advertisements and affects the device's performance.

Aesthetics: The visual appeal and design elements of an accessory, focusing on its appearance and beauty.

App development: Is the process of developing software for specific operating systems, such as iOS and iPadOS.

App Icon Size: The option to resize app icons on the home screen for better visibility and interaction.

App Performance: The speed and responsiveness of applications running on the iPad.

App Store: A website that hosts a store where customers can purchase and download iPad apps.

App Switcher: A tool that displays recently used apps for quick and easy access.

App Tracking Transparency: A feature that allows users to control which apps can track their data across other apps and websites.

Apple Developer Resources: Online tools, documentation, and support provided by Apple for app developers.

Apple Ecosystem: The integrated ecosystem of services and products from Apple that operate in unison with one another.

Apple Pay: Is a payment service that enables users of their iPad or iPhone to complete safe transactions in shops, online, and within apps.

Apple Watch: A wearable device that can be paired with the iPad to track health parameters like heart rate, exercise, and sleep.

Apps: are computer programs created for mobile devices that carry out certain functions or offer enjoyment.

AssistiveTouch: A feature that provides an on-screen menu for accessing essential functions without physical buttons.

Augmented Reality (AR) : Is a method that places digital information over the real world to enhance the user's perception of reality.

Auto Unlock: This feature enables users to utilize Touch ID or Face ID on their iPad or iPhone to automatically unlock their Mac.

Battery life: The amount of time the iPad can function between charges.

Battery-saving features: Features that optimize power consumption and prolong battery life in a Bluetooth keyboard or mouse are known as battery-saving features.

Blockchain Technology: Various applications are made possible by the decentralized and secure digital ledger technology known as blockchain.

Bluetooth: Enables the transmission of data across short distances via wireless technology.

Booking.com app: It is a well-known website for booking hotels, and it offers a wide range of housing options and reservation methods.

Braided cables: Braided cables have a woven outer covering that adds durability and resistance to wear.

Apps for Brain Training: Apps that provide exercises and activities to challenge and develop cognitive ability.

Calendar App: Apple Calendar is a pre-installed app for the iPad that allows users to manage events, appointments, and schedules.

Calorie Counter Apps: Apps that assist users in tracking their daily calorie intake and food consumption in order to support weight management and healthy eating.

Cases: iPad protective cases that protect the device while also adding functionality.

Closing an App: To exit an app, swipe up from the bottom of the screen, pause in the center, and then swipe it off the screen.

Other Apple Devices Compatibility: iPads' ability to interface and share data with other Apple goods.

Connectivity: Internet access options include Wi-Fi and cellular data.

Content recommendations: Digital content recommendations based on the user's likes and habits.

Contextually Aware Technology: Technology that recognizes and adapts to the user's context.

Continuity: A group of technologies, like Handoff, Instant Hotspot, and Universal Clipboard, that promote fluid interactions between Apple devices, allowing users to operate smoothly across many devices.

Contrast: Is the difference in brightness between objects or elements on a screen that can affect vision and eye strain.

Convenience: The level of ease and practicality provided by an attachment when using the iPad.

Copy and Paste: The process of copying and pasting text or content into another area.

Culture Trip App: An app that offers city tours and personalized travel recommendations for a number of destinations.

Cutting-edge technologies: are cutting-edge innovations that are at the forefront of technology.

Data Breach: Unauthorized access to or disclosure of sensitive data.

Data privacy: Is the protection of personal and sensitive information from unauthorized access and usage.

Decentralized Technologies: Systems that operate without a central authority, as seen in blockchain technology.

Designers and Artists: With strong drawing and design tools, the iPad and Apple Pencil have changed digital artwork and graphic design.

Device Integration: The smooth connectivity and interoperability of multiple devices.

Device Switching: Switching between devices while preserving a consistent user experience.

Digital Asset Management: Digital assets, such as photographs and documents, are to be organized, stored, and retrieved.

Digital Environment: The digital space in which users interact with technology and content.

Digital Healthcare: The integration of technology in healthcare to monitor, track, and improve health and wellness.

Digital Payments: Transactions conducted electronically using technologies like Apple Pay or other online payment services.

Downloading an App: The steps involved in downloading and installing an app on the iPad from the App Store.

DPI (Dots Per Inch): An assessment of a mouse cursor's sensitivity and accuracy.

Drawing Apps: Software that allows users to produce digital artwork and drawings.

Ebooks: are digital books available for reading on iPads and other portable devices.

Educational Apps: Software applications designed to provide learning resources and aid in educational activities.

Educational Games: Interactive games designed to enhance learning and problem-solving skills.

Email communication: Is the sending of communications via electronic mail between people.

Emergency SOS: Is a feature on the iPad that allows users to send emergency alerts and disclose their location to designated emergency contacts in critical situations.

Encryption: Protects data against illegal access by encoding it.

Ergonomic design: The consideration of human factors and user comfort in the design of an accessory.

External Drives, or SSDs: are storage devices that can be connected externally to the iPad to expand its storage capacity.

Face ID: Is a facial recognition technology that enables users to use their faces to unlock their iPads.

Face-to-Face Encounters: In-person meetings or interactions between individuals.

Files App: A pre-installed app on the iPad, Files is a central hub for managing files stored on the device and cloud storage services.

Find My iPad: Is an Apple feature that helps locate lost or stolen iPads and protects them from unauthorized access.

Fitness Objectives: Specific goals related to physical health and exercise that users can monitor and track using health and fitness apps.

Flash drives: For rapid data transfer and backup, tiny and portable storage devices.

Focus Mode: Is a customization tool that filters notifications and app alerts based on selected contexts.

Guided Access: A setting that confines the iPad to a single app in order to avoid unintentional exits or unwanted entry.

iPad Settings for Travel: Adjusting iPad settings for best travel use, including data roaming and offline functionality.

iPad: A brand of tablet computers developed and manufactured by Apple Inc.

Malware: Malicious software that can harm the iPad and compromise data security.

Mind-Building Apps: Applications focused on brain training and cognitive exercises to improve mental abilities.

Phishing: Is a deceptive technique that involves sending emails or texts to trick people into divulging personal information or making unauthorized purchases.

Ransomware: Is a type of malware that encrypts files and demands payment to decrypt them.

Scams: False attempts to deceive customers into disclosing private information or sending money to a false account, such as fake lottery prizes or tech support scams.

Sidecar: A feature that enables users to connect their iPad to their Mac desktop and use it as a second monitor or a drawing tablet with support for the Apple Pencil.

Software Updates: Apple releases updates on a regular basis to improve the functionality and security of their products.

Split View: The iPad's Split View multitasking function enables users to run two apps simultaneously on the screen.

Spoofing: Posing as trustworthy organizations to lead users to believe in false sources.

Spyware: Is software that secretly records user actions and information about the device without the user's awareness.

Technical Details: Specific technical information about a device, system, or technology.

Technical Setup: Configuring and setting up devices and services for optimal performance.

Touch ID: Enables users to unlock their iPad with their fingerprint thanks to fingerprint recognition technology.

Two-Factor Authentication (2FA): An additional layer of security that requires users to enter a verification code, which is often sent to a trusted device or phone number, while checking in with their Apple ID.

Uninstalling an Application: Removing an app from the iPad is as simple as touching and holding its symbol until it jiggles, then tapping the "X" in the top-left corner and confirming the deletion.

Updating an Application: Keeping programs up-to-date by activating automatic updates or manually checking the App Store for updates.

Virtual reality (VR): Is a technology that produces a virtual environment, which is often experienced through a head-mounted display and provides a completely immersive experience.

Virtual Worlds: Immersive digital environments created through VR technology.

Vision Impairment: A condition where a person's ability to see is reduced or impaired, leading to difficulty reading or viewing digital content.

Visual Schedules: Visual representations of daily activities and tasks to assist individuals in understanding routines.

Voice Assistants: Voice-activated smart assistants enabled by AI that carry out tasks.

Voice Commands: The ability to control the iPad and perform tasks using spoken words and commands.

Voice-first Interactions: Interacting with devices using natural language voice commands.

Widgets: Aspects that can be customized and are located on the iPad home screen, offering rapid access to app functionality and real-time information.

Wireless Charging Pad: A device that wirelessly charges compatible devices like the iPad.

Wireless Charging Station: A location or surface where wireless charging pads can be placed to charge devices.

Wireless Charging: Charging devices without the need for wired connections using wireless charging pads or stations.

REFERENCES

Apple. (2019). iOS - Health. Apple. https://www.apple.com/ios/health/

Apple ID - Official Apple Support. (n.d.). Support.apple.com. https://support.apple.com/en-ph/apple-id

Atwin. (n.d.). *How to Set Up an iPad for Seniors.* Ohana is family. https://www.ohanaisfamily.com/blog/how-to-set-up-an-ipad-for-seniors

Baker, R. (2022, November 8). *10 Best iPad Productivity Apps For You.* TASK. https://www.ntaskmanager.com/blog/best-ipad-productivity-app/

Consultants, S. (2018, November 19). *What is an iPad? What can you actually use an iPad for?* Phonebox. https://phonebox.com.mt/blog/what-is-an-ipad-what-can-you-actually-use-an-ipad-for/

D'Angelo, M. (n.d.). *How to Use an iPad for Business.* Business News Daily. https://www.businessnewsdaily.com/6105-how-to-use-ipad-business.html

Delfino, D., & John, S. (2021, October 21). *How To Write And Edit Amazon Reviews, And Find Or Delete Your Reviews.* Business Insider. https://www.businessinsider.com/guides/tech/my-amazon-reviews?r=US&IR=T

Duffy, J. (2023, March 3). *The Best Travel Apps for 2022.* PCMAG. https://www.pcmag.com/picks/best-travel-apps

Evans, J. (2019, April 15). *12+ essential iPad productivity tips.* Computerworld. https://www.computerworld.com/article/3388309/12-essential-ipad-productivity-tips.html

Helper, T. T. (2020, August 17). *The Best iPad accessories for seniors.* The Tech Helper. https://www.thetechhelper.com/best-ipad-accessories-seniors/

How to back up your iPhone or iPad with iCloud. (2022, September 12). Apple Support. https://support.apple.com/en-ph/HT211228

Hoyt, J. (2023, July 27). Our [year] *List of Apps for Seniors and the Elderly.* SeniorLiving.org. https://www.seniorliving.org/cell-phone/apps/

Idowu. (2023, May 25). *Best education apps for iPhone and iPad in 2023.* IGeeksBlog. https://www.igeeksblog.com/best-education-apps-for-iphone-ipad/

iPad - Compare Models. (n.d.). Apple (Philippines). https://www.apple.com/ph/ipad/compare/

iPad - Why iPad. (n.d.). Apple (Philippines). https://www.apple.com/ph/ipad/why-ipad/

Khanna, G. (2023, March 7). *Top 12 iOS App Development Trends You Can't Ignore (2023).* APPWRK IT Solutions. https://appwrk.com/ios-app-development-trends

Meeks, J. H. (2017). *Using an Apple iPad and Communication Application to Increase Communication in Students with Autism Spectrum Disorder.* Georgia Educational Researcher, 14(1). https://doi.org/10.20429/ger.2017.140106

Papiewski, J. (2012). *What Are the Functions of the iPad?* Chron. https://smallbusiness.chron.com/functions-ipad-55280.html

Recognize and avoid phishing messages, phony support calls, and other scams. (n.d.). Apple Support. https://support.apple.com/en-us/HT204759

Rees, K. (2021, December 19). *The Top 6 Specs to Check Before Buying a New Tablet.* MUO. https://www.makeuseof.com/specs-check-before-buying-new-tablet/

Robertson, N. (n.d.). *IPads for Sawnee Sawnee ElementaryApple &.* What is iPad? As most of you know, is a line of tablet computer created by Apple, Inc. The user interface is. - ppt download. Slideplayer. https://slideplayer.com/slide/8682539

Send and reply to messages on iPad. (n.d.). Apple Support. https://support.apple.com/en-ph/guide/ipad/ipad99acb44a/ipados

Shaik, A. I. (2021, August 29). *Tablet Buying Guide 2021: These Are the Features You Should Look Out For.* Onsitego. https://onsitego.com/blog/tablet-buying-guide-2020/

Snuggs, N. (n.d.). *10 Inspirational Tech Quotes.* Kerridge Commercial Systems Blog. https://blog.kerridgecs.com/10-inspirational-tech-quotes

Top iPad Health & Fitness apps on the App Store (US). (n.d.). Apple App

Store. https://apps.apple.com/us/charts/ipad/health-fitness-apps/6013

Top iPhone Travel apps on the App Store (US). (n.d.). Apple App Store. https://apps.apple.com/us/charts/iphone/travel-apps/6003

Turner, J. (2023, January 5). *Which iPad Should I Buy? | 2023 iPad Guide.* Tech.co. https://tech.co/tablets-ipads/which-ipad-should-buy

Use Continuity to connect your Mac, iPhone, iPad, and Apple Watch. (2022, October 24). Apple Support. https://support.apple.com/en-ph/HT204681

IMAGE REFERENCES

Banerjee, S. (2021). *Black and white laptop computer* [Image]. Unsplash. https://unsplash.com/photos/8dOk8JVESxY

Cottonbro studio. (2020). *Person Wearing Silver Aluminum Case Apple Watch With White Sport Band* [Image]. Pexels. https://www.pexels.com/photo/person-wearing-silver-aluminum-case-apple-watch-with-white-sport-band-5081424/

Danilevich, O. (2020). *Back to School Flatlay* [Image]. Pexels. https://www.pexels.com/photo/back-to-school-flatlay-5088024/

Diedryreyes3456. (2021). [Image]. Pixabay. https://pixabay.com/photos/email-website-technology-gmail-6520447/

GoodNotes. (2022). *a tablet with a screen* [Image]. Unsplash. https://unsplash.com/photos/ypyf9CO__0k

Jordan, B. (2021). *Close Up Shot of a Smartphone Screen* [Image]. Pexels. https://www.pexels.com/photo/close-up-shot-of-a-smartphone-screen-7568293/

Kétyi, B. (2019). *LOCUS is a smart city and IOT mobile application* [Image]. Unsplash. https://unsplash.com/photos/byoBbHSIP5U

Kumar, D. (2020) [Image]. Unsplash. https://unsplash.com/photos/36X1uC8FszI

LinkedIn Sales Solutions. (2017). *Man holding tablet computer* [Image]. Unsplash. https://unsplash.com/photos/UK1N66KUkMk

Nickson, R. (2019). *Black iPad* [Image]. Unsplash. https://unsplash.com/photos/hLgYtX0rPgw

Niekverlaan. (2020). *Person Holding White Ipad Displaying Man And Woman* [Image]. Pexels. https://www.pexels.com/photo/person-holding-white-ipad-displaying-man-and-woman-5970871/

White IPad. (2016). *White Ipad* [Image]. Pexels. https://www.pexels.com/photo/white-ipad-38271/

Sheldon, J. (2017). *Closeup photo of turned on iPad with rack on table* [Image]. Unsplash. https://unsplash.com/photos/6MT4_Ut8a3Y

Shypka, T. (2017). *Using Web on iPad* [Image]. Unsplash. https://unsplash.com/photos/iFSvn82XfGo

Sinn, A. (2020). *Headphones on iPad with Apple Music* [Image]. Unsplash. https://unsplash.com/photos/85Ki4n1dsZw

Sorenson, J. (2018). *Turned on Ipad* [Image]. Pexels. https://www.pexels.com/photo/turned-on-ipad-1334597/

Underworld, E. (2021). *A tablet with the words mental health matters on it* [Image]. Unsplash. https://unsplash.com/photos/Ko3EMBFggok

Wadhwa, M. (2021). *Black android smartphone on white table* [Image]. Unsplash. https://unsplash.com/photos/Uq8wqsbd7Wk

Watel, S. (2019). *Man holding Apple pencil* [Image]. Unsplash. https://unsplash.com/photos/4wY6p2F2jeE

Zagórski, T. (2019). *Black tablet computer with gray portable keyboard on brown wooden coffee table* [Image]. Unsplash. https://unsplash.com/photos/-MJftweKIJc